NICE, CANNES & MONTE CARLO

POCKET GUIDE

Walking Eye
mobile app

Discover the world's best destinations with the Insight Guides Walking Eye app, available to download for free in the App Store and Google Play.

The container app provides easy access to fantastic free content on events and activities taking place in your current location or chosen destination, with the possibility of booking, as well as the regularly-updated Insight Guides travel blog: Inspire Me. In addition, you can purchase curated, premium destination guides through the app, which feature local highlights, hotel, bar, restaurant and shopping listings, an A to Z of practical information and more. Or purchase and download Insight Guides eBooks straight to your device.

TOP 10 ATTRACTIONS

COLLINE DU CHÂTEAU
Nothing remains of the medieval citadel, but glorious views of Nice abound. See page 34.

MOUGINS
This picture-perfect hilltop village is a must-visit for foodies. See page 80.

MUSÉE MATISSE
Nice is home to this unmissable collection from all stages of the artist's career. See page 50.

LA CROISETTE
The animated seafront promenade at Cannes is perfect for watching the world go by. See page 53.

PROMENADE DES ANGLAIS
The legendary footpath epitomises the elegance of Belle Epoque Nice. See page 40.

CASINO DE MONTE CARLO
The ultimate symbol of Monaco glamour since 1863. See page 65.

MARCHÉ FORVILLE
Cannes' colourful feast of wonderful Riviera produce. See page 56.

PALAIS PRINCIER
Monaco's hilltop palace is compact and quaint with wonderful views over the coast. See page 72.

VIEUX NICE
An atmospheric Italianate maze of narrow streets and coloured campaniles. See page 28.

ILES DE LÉRINS
Escape the Cannes crowds and make the trip across the bay to these forested islands. See page 61.

A PERFECT DAY

9.00am

Breakfast
Instead of having breakfast in your hotel, head to Café Lenôtre (63 rue d'Antibes, www. lenotre.com) for a croissant and a *crème* (milky coffee) or, if you're on a tight budget, grab a pavement seat outside one of the boulangeries on rue Meynadier.

9.30am

At the market
Rub shoulders with top chefs while you check out the wonderful local produce – look out for courgette flowers and Mediterranean fish – at Marché Forville, one of the most animated and colourful markets on the Riviera.

11.00am

Retail therapy
Browse the high street and designer shops along rue d'Antibes and rue du Commandant André to pick out something stylish to wear for your night out on the town.

10.00am

Up the hill
Walk up cobbled rue St-Antoine in Cannes' old town, Le Suquet, and head to the Musée de la Castre to see its collections of primitive art and musical instruments. On the way, don't forget to admire the views across the bay.

12.30pm

Lunch
Take the boat from the port over to Ile Saint-Honorat and enjoy a waterside lunch with panoramic views across the coast at La Tonnelle restaurant (http://tonnelle-abbayedelerins.fr). Visit the Abbaye de Lérins, home to 30 Cistercian monks, and buy some of their wine, liqueurs or lavender honey to take home.

IN **CANNES**

7.00pm

Apéro time
Once you've showered and changed back at the hotel, take a stroll along La Croisette, admiring the luxury clothes and jewellery shops on the way, and turn into rue des Frères Pradignac for an apéritif on the terrace at the bar, For You.

10.30pm

On the town
There's only one place to be seen partying in Cannes and that's Le Bâoli at the eastern end of La Croisette – at least, if the doormen think you're cool enough to get in. Otherwise, try the Sun7 Bar on rue Gérard-Monod.

3.00pm

On the beach
Back on the continent, rent a sunbed at Zplage, the private beach of the five-star Hôtel Martinez and one of the swankiest places to sun yourself on the French Riviera. If sipping cocktails alongside celebs and the international jetset is out of your reach, head to the sandy public beach, Plage du Midi, west of the port.

8.30pm

Dinner is served
Take your table at Table 22 (www.restaurantmantel. com) in rue St-Antoine to try some delicious Mediterranean cuisine cooked by Noël Mantel and his Dutch wife. Fish fans can also head to Astoux et Brun (see page 110) near the port to savour some seafood.

CONTENTS

INTRODUCTION

Nice, Cannes, Monaco. The three names alone evoke many of the myths of the Côte d'Azur, each endowed with grandiose architecture and spectacular natural settings: the Baie de Cannes with the backdrop of the red Estérel mountains to the west, Nissa la Bella (Beautiful Nice) sitting on the glorious curve of the Baie des Anges, or the crazy piled-up tower blocks of Monaco, clustered between sea and the white limestone crags of the Alpine foothills.

The gentle Mediterranean climate made the French Riviera a magnet for the aristocratic winter visitors of the Belle Epoque, and its quality of light attracted Matisse, Picasso, Bonnard, de Staël and countless other artists during the 20th century. Today, mild sunny winters interspersed by just a few chilly days, crisp spring sunlight and the guarantee of hot summers with an azure-blue sea continue to draw tourists from the world over.

These are active year-round cities. Nice is the administrative capital of the Alpes-Maritimes *département*, with a dynamic cultural scene, a growing university, a large services sector and a nearby hi-tech science park at Sophia Antipolis. Cannes glories in film-star kudos yet resounds to a busy congress schedule that is fuelled by a non-stop succession of TV producers, music industry magnates, property developers and experts in all things luxurious (the luxury shopping, tourism and yachting industries all descend here for their trade fairs). Monaco's casinos now merely play a supporting role to the profits generated by luxury spas and financial and banking services.

ARCHITECTURAL HERITAGE

All three cities have an architectural heritage begging to be discovered. The late 16th- and 17th-century expansion of Nice below the Colline du Château gave Vieux Nice pretty much the Italianate Baroque face it still has today, with pastel-coloured campaniles, imposing Genoese-style palaces, such as Palais Lascaris, and richly decorated churches, like the Cathédrale Sainte-Réparate, the Gésu and the Miséricorde and Sainte-Rita chapels, where relatively sober facades hide interiors awash with the carving, stucco and fake marble,

Vieux Nice

sculpted saints and cherubs, sunbursts and barley-sugar columns that marked the Catholic Counter-Reformation.

Above all, the late 19th and early 20th centuries shaped the architectural flavour of the cities, when the Riviera developed as a chic winter destination for the European aristocracy. The Belle Epoque was marked by eclectic decoration – neo-Gothic, neo-Renaissance, neoclassical and neo-Louis XIII were all utilised in banks, hotels, casinos, villas and churches. The winter gardens of Hôtel Hermitage in Monte Carlo and the Art Deco facade of the Palais de la Méditerranée in Nice give today's visitors a hint of what life was previously like, at least for the wealthy, in the cities' heyday.

CITIES OF CONTRAST

Perhaps part of the appeal of all three destinations and one of the reasons they continue to fascinate are their apparent paradoxes.

Palatial seafront hotels contrast with the charm of narrow village streets; luxury yachts drop anchor alongside the few remaining *pointu* fishing boats; shop windows displaying diamond necklaces contrast with the stalls at daily food markets overflowing with local produce.

Nice combines all the allure of an elegant seaside resort with the urban pulse of a working city. With a population of 344,000, it is France's fifth city and heart of a conurbation of nearly 1,000,000, with Roman remains, fine architecture, world-class art museums, wide-ranging shops and a vibrant culinary scene. Long the capital of the quasi-independent Comté de Nice, later a cosmopolitan winter destination, Nice offers the charm of the narrow *ruelles* of its Old Town and the elegance of the planned streets of the new. In Cannes, the *département*'s third city (after Nice and Antibes), with a population of over 73,000, an undeniably snobby aspect of extortionately priced beaches and posey restaurants coexists with the more popular charm of its covered market, the Provençal village atmosphere of Le Suquet and the democracy of the evening stroll along La Croisette.

In the city of Monaco, the fascinating modernity of skyscraper architecture and daring land reclamation schemes (the principality has grown in area by 25 percent since World War II) contrasts with the seeming anachronism of one of the world's tiniest monarchies: ostensibly a constitutional monarchy since 1911, signs of royalty are everywhere in this highly autocratic state. The 8,800 Monégasque citizens may elect the Conseil National which consists of 24 parliamentarians every five years, but the real sense of power stays with the Sovereign Prince, who signs all of the ordinances and nominates (and these are subject to approval by France), the Minister of State and also five other members of the government.

Nice's tramway

IMAGE MAKEOVER

Not everything is rosy when everyone wants to live in the sun. Urban sprawl has disfigured much of the coast. Pressure for land and flats bought by often absent tax exiles makes Monaco far too expensive for most of its employees to live there. There's a shortage of housing, too, in Cannes, where people prefer to let flats at high prices to festival-goers, congress clientele and tourists than to the local population; while the contrasts between rich and poor are striking in Nice's housing estates and the villas of Mont Boron.

But Nice is undergoing a renaissance. After a period at the end of the 20th century when it was stricken by its reputation for financial corruption, prostitution rings, an association with far-right politics and an image as the dowager of the Riviera, Nice has emerged in a refreshed mood, the population rejuvenated by a growing number of students and the international set who have colonised Vieux Nice. Stimulated by low-cost flights and the influx of pleasure-seekers from the east, Nice once again has the sort of cosmopolitan feel it had in the Belle Epoque, even if it is no longer the playground of the aristocracy. The urban fabric, too, is experiencing a renewal: streets have been cleaned, buildings are being renovated and a new sense of civic pride was symbolised by the repaving of place Masséna for the opening of the T1 tramway line in 2007. Part of the T2 line was inaugurated in mid-2018 and its remaining part is scheduled to start operating in mid-2019. The T3 and T4 lines are also planned.

Monaco, too, is trying to change its image. Somerset Maugham, who owned a house at Saint-Jean-Cap-Ferrat, called the principality 'a sunny place for shady people', and after the ignominy of its being put on the OECD blacklist of tax havens, Prince Albert II has brought in a new team of councillors and vowed to make banking practices more transparent.

A GREENER FUTURE

Perhaps the element that most typifies the new century is environmental awareness. In Monaco, Albert II has set up the Prince Albert II Foundation (www.fpa2.com) to protect the environment and encourage sustainable development in both Monaco and the rest of the world through funding a wide range of projects, one of which is to protect the endangered Bluefin tuna – you won't find it on any restaurant menu in the principality. On the initiative of Christian Estrosi, mayor of Nice since 2008, a territorial project called 'Eco-Vallée' was in the pipeline, however it was sadly killed off in 2017, but will hopefully be rekindled in the future.

Cannes now also has a wide-ranging charter for sustainable development, from protection of the natural spaces of the Iles de Lérins and La Croix des Gardes to stabilisation of the beaches, water conservation, energy-efficient street lighting, new cycle lanes and electric buses.

A BRIEF HISTORY

Although just a few kilometres apart, Nice, Cannes and Monaco have had contrasting histories, often poised on opposing sides: Cannes as part of Provence and, later, France; Nice long an independent city state linked to Genoa and the house of Savoy; and Monaco, a tiny autocratic principality.

BEGINNINGS

During the 4th century BC, Phocaean Greeks from Massilia (Marseille) founded trading posts named Nikaia (probably after *nike* for victory), roughly on the site of what is now Vieux Nice, and Monoikos (Monaco). However, traces of human settlement go back much earlier, to Terra Amata at the foot of Mont Boron, where a tribe of elephant-hunters set up camp some 400,000 years ago.

Nearby Lazaret Cave, thought to have been inhabited 170,000 years ago, is still being excavated.

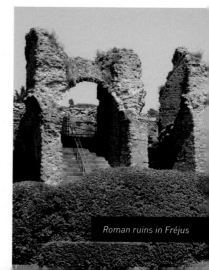

Roman ruins in Fréjus

In the 1st century BC, the Romans defeated the Vediantii tribe and took over its hill settlement, renaming it Cemenelum (now Cimiez), on the strategic Via Julia Augusta between Italy and Spain, making it capital of Alpes

Maritimae province in AD 69. Cemenelum reached its peak in the 3rd century. Traces of the city, with three bathing establishments and a huge amphitheatre, can be seen at the Cimiez archaeological site.

Christianity gradually spread along the coast, and in 410 a monastery was founded on the island of Lérina (now Ile Saint-Honorat), which acquired extensive influence and territory (including Cannes) on the mainland.

With the fall of the Roman Empire in 476, the region was invaded first by Barbarians from the East, then Saracens from North Africa, but it was the Franks who triumphed, establishing the Carolingian Empire, which stretched from western Germany to northern Spain and Italy. When Charlemagne's empire was divided in 843, Provence, nominally controlled by the Holy Roman Empire, was in effect an independent principality.

COUNTS VERSUS CONSULATS

In 972 Guillaume the Liberator drove the Saracens from their stronghold at La Garde Freinet in the Maures, bringing new prosperity to Provence, although the coast continued to suffer from marauding pirates. Fiercely independent Nice opposed the more centralised rule of the Provençal count and in 1144 established a Consulat, a sort of mini-republic whereby the town was administered by four elected consuls.

Count Ramon Berenger V, ruling from Aix-en-Provence since 1215, was determined to unify Provence and get rid of the consulates. In 1229 he invaded Nice, which had put itself under Genoese protection, and installed officials to administer the town. The count married all his daughters to kings or future kings: Marguerite to Louis IX of France, Eléonore to Henry III of England, Sanchia to Richard, earl of Cornwall, and Béatrice of Provence to Charles of Anjou, who thus inherited the title

The 17th-century Château Grimaldi in Antibes

count of Provence in 1246, soon adding the kingdom of Sicily and Naples as well.

Meanwhile, Genoa had taken possession of Monaco and begun building a fortress. With Genoa caught up in the wars between the Guelph (pro-pope) and Ghibelline (pro-German emperor) factions, many of its noble families took refuge in eastern Provence, among them assorted branches of the Grimaldi family. In 1297, François Grimaldi, disguised as a monk, seized power as self-styled Seigneur of Monaco, establishing a new ruling dynasty (although it took the title of principality only in 1641).

Early 13th-century Nice prospered with the growth of important monasteries, and the town began to spread below the castle hill between the River Paillon and the sea. When Jeanne, Countess of Provence and Queen of Naples, chose Louis of Anjou, brother of French king Charles V, as her heir, rather than her cousin Charles III of Duras, Provence was divided. In 1382, Jeanne was

Good King René ruled from 1434–80

assassinated near Naples, leading to a six-year civil war between pro-Anjou Marseille and pro-Duras Nice. In 1388 Nice submitted to Savoyard protection rather than that of Anjou, under the Dédition of Nice. Henceforth, Nice's fortunes were associated with Italy and the Holy Roman Empire, while Cannes on the western side of the River Var remained part of Provence, and Monaco – generally – sided with the French. With its sovereign conveniently far away, Nice enjoyed a new independence and prosperity from trade (essentially agricultural produce) with Italy, and an influx of Italian settlers bringing a culture distinguished by art and architecture, but the relationship also meant 400 years of on-off conflict with France.

Italians also settled elsewhere on the Riviera, brought in by landlords to cultivate land abandoned since the Black Death; while in a late flourishing of Gothic style, an artistic school grew up in Nice around the Bréa family (see box).

Power struggles intensified after 1481 when Provence was absorbed into the French kingdom. In the early 16th century, Nice thwarted the ambitions of François I, who hoped that he, rather than Charles I of Spain (future Emperor Charles V) would be elected Holy Roman Emperor. In 1538 Pope Paul III initiated negotiations between the French king, who stayed in the fortress at Villeneuve-Loubet, and Emperor Charles V, who resided at Villefranche-sur-Mer. The Treaty of Nice brought short-lived peace, but in 1543 the allied troops of François I and Turkish Sultan Suleiman the Magnificent besieged the city. According to local legend, on 15 August washerwoman Catherine Ségurane grabbed a Turkish standard and pushed back the invaders. Although the lower town was sacked, the castle hill held out until relieved by Charles V's forces. Ségurane has gone down in local memory as a symbol of Niçois courage and feisty independence – although it is not certain that she ever existed.

WARS AND REVOLUTION

The expansion of Nice accelerated in the 17th century, when Emmanuel Philibert I converted the hilltop town into a bastioned citadel, and forced the population to move below, endowing Vieux Nice with Italianate Baroque style, with richly decorated

○ LUDOVICO BRÉA

Louis or Ludovico Bréa was the leading figure of an artistic school that flourished in the Comté de Nice during the late 15th and early 16th century. Born in Nice in around 1450 to a family of barrel-makers who lived in rue Barillerie, he was soon carrying out commissions for churches and religious confraternities across the region. His powerful paintings mix the emotion of late Provençal Gothic with the discovery of perspective of the Italian Renaissance. You can see altar-pieces by him (as well as works by his family and followers, including Antoine Bréa, François Bréa, Giovanni Balaisin and Giovanni Canevesio) in several churches in Nice, Monaco, the southern Alpine valleys and across the Italian border.

The Casino on the pier at Nice

churches and imposing Genoese-style palaces.

France besieged Nice again in 1691 and in 1705 during the War of Spanish Succession, when Savoyard Nice sided with the Habsburgs against French claims to the Spanish throne; in 1706 the citadel was razed, on the orders of Louis XIV, and this time not rebuilt. With Savoyard rule re-established, in 1782–92 King Victor-Amédée III of Sardinia laid out a grandiose arcaded square, the Piazza Vittoria (now place Garibaldi), at the entrance to town on the new route from his capital Turin, and began digging the new Port Lympia.

With the peasantry and bourgeoisie submerged by taxes to finance wars, and poor harvests leading to bread shortages, the people of Provence were active participants in the French Revolution; many of the aristocracy fled across the Var to take refuge in Nice. In 1792, the revolutionary Armée du Midi invaded Nice and Monaco, which remained under French rule until 1814, when the Treaty of Paris returned Nice to Sardinia-Piedmont and restored the Prince of Monaco to his throne.

WINTER VISITORS

The 18th century saw the beginning of winter visitors from northern Europe. Lord and Lady Cavendish stayed in Nice in 1731, followed by other British aristocrats, among them the

Duke of York in 1764, and by novelist Tobias Smollett, who described the town and its people in his *Travels Through France and Italy* (1766), admiring the remains of Cemenelum, treating Nice's 'slovenly' maids, 'greedy' shopkeepers and 'lazy' artisans with characteristic condescension and advocating the benefits of sea air for the lungs. By the 1780s some 300 British visitors wintered in Nice, settling to the west of town in a district they dubbed Newborough. In 1822, Reverend Lewis Way opened a public subscription for building a new seafront footpath, actually an employment exercise after a harsh winter, soon called the chemin des Anglais (renamed promenade des Anglais in 1844).

In 1834 British Lord Chancellor Henry Brougham was forced to overnight in Cannes because an outbreak of cholera prevented him crossing the border. He liked it so much he stayed, buying a plot of land and building the Villa Eléonore (named after his daughter) with gardens down to the sea. Cannes was transformed from a fishing village into an aristocratic watering hole for the English, who built elegant villas, mainly on the western side of town in the Quartier de la Croix des Gardes – fresh air and fine views being more important than proximity to the sea. Hotels were built for visitors and a veritable property market developed: Sir Thomas Woolfield was known for building extravagant residences, then selling them on, while in 1864 his former gardener, John Taylor, founded an estate agency that still exists today.

Royal patronage

In 1897 and 1899, Queen Victoria spent several months at the Hôtel Excelsior Régina in Cimiez, built in her honour, where she occupied the entire west wing. Travelling as Lady Balmoral, the queen socialised with European aristocracy (many of them her relations) and visited the town in a cart drawn by a donkey.

REUNIFICATION AND REGENERATION

In return for Napoleon III's support against Austria in the unification of Italy, King Victor Emmanuel II agreed to hand back Savoie and the Comté de Nice, confirmed by a vast majority in a referendum in April 1860. The population of the city nearly tripled between 1861 and 1911, boosted by the arrival of the railway in 1864, with people drawn in by the booming economy of Second Empire France. The expansion of the New Town continued in the Quartier des Musiciens, Les Baumettes and Cimiez, where the visit of Queen Victoria confirmed Nice as a fashionable destination. English aristocrats were joined by pleasure-seeking Russians, who built fairytale villas and the Russian Orthodox cathedral.

A treaty in 1861 also confirmed the attachment of Menton and Roquebrune, which had broken off from Monaco in the 1848 revolution. In search of new revenue, Prince Charles III turned to gambling, awarding the concession to run the Casino (banned in both neighbouring France and Italy) to businessman François Blanc, founder of the Société des Bains de Mer de Monaco. Blanc soon added the Hôtel de Paris to accommodate the gamblers and called in Parisian architect Charles Garnier to design an opera house, adjoining the Casino, giving rise to a whole new district, Monte Carlo.

In the early 20th century, grand hotels went up along the seafront promenade in Cannes, and from 1922 the Calais Méditerranée Express, better known as the Train Bleu, brought British visitors direct from Calais to the Côte d'Azur. Americans introduced the new pleasures of sunbathing and waterskiing, and in 1931 the summer season was born when the grand hotels of Juan-les-Pins and Cannes stayed open in summer for the first time.

Avant-garde artists, musicians and writers – including Matisse, Picasso, Stravinsky, Diaghilev, Ernest Hemingway,

Henry Miller and Gertrude Stein – also colonised the south, drawn by the southern light and the attractions of the new Mediterranean society.

WAR AND POST-WAR

During World War II, the Alpes-Maritimes was part of so-called Unoccupied France under the Vichy regime, until occupied by Italian troops in November 1942. They were replaced in September 1943 by

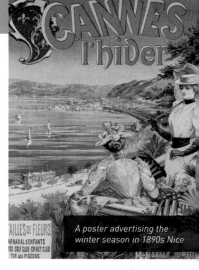

A poster advertising the winter season in 1890s Nice

German troops after the fall of Mussolini, and liberated in August 1944 by Allied troops from North Africa. The first Cannes Film Festival (see page 55) – originally planned for 1939 but postponed due to the war – took place in 1946, heralding a glamorous new image for Cannes – and for Monaco, when film star Grace Kelly married Prince Rainier III in 1956, with Sir Alfred Hitchcock as their witness.

The post-war period saw all three cities expand enormously, especially Nice, with immigration from North Africa and the return of the *pieds-noirs* (the white colonial population) in the 1960s, following Algerian independence. At the same time there was a change in the type of tourism, already augmented when working people first received paid holidays in 1936, and holidays in the southern sun were no longer the preserve of aristocrats and artists. The birth of mass tourism led to widescale construction all along the coast.

Twentieth-century Nice was also marked by the long reign of mayor Jean Médecin, elected 1928–43 and re-elected from 1947–65, at which point his son, Jacques, succeeded him. Under Jacques Médecin, Nice gained its modern art museum, new theatre, casinos, and the Arenas business district; the town also became the creative centre of a dynamic artistic movement, the Ecole de Nice (see page 39). Adored by many Niçois, Médecin veered close to extreme right politics and was suspected of financial embezzlement, before escaping to Uruguay in 1990 to avoid corruption charges. There (after extradition to France and a brief spell in jail) he died in 1998. In the 21st century, Nice has many environmental and cultural projects in progress but sadly its momentum was brought to an abrupt halt on 14th July 2016 when an Islamic terrorist ploughed a truck into a crowd gathered on the promenade des Anglais for the Bastille Day celebrations, killing 86 people and injuring hundreds. Hopefully, the 8th FIFA Women's World Cup to be held in mid-2019 across nine French cities, including Nice, will generate more optimistic moods, just as the UEFA Euro Football Championship did back in 2016.

Under Prince Rainier III, Monaco began to take on its present form, with a booming banking sector, skyscrapers replacing 19th-century villas, and an entire district, Fontvieille, constructed on land reclaimed from the sea. Amid suspicions of money laundering, the tax haven's relationship with France and the EU is not always easy, and Prince Albert II, who succeeded in 2005, has promised greater transparency. In 2011 the principality had plenty to celebrate when Albert II married South African former Olympic swimmer Charlene Wittstock, and again in 2014 when she gave birth to twins Gabriella and Jacques, the heir apparent to the Monégasque throne. In 2016, Monaco and the EU signed the tax transparency agreement under which they started exchanging financial information of residents in 2018.

HISTORICAL LANDMARKS

350 BC Phocaeans from Marseille set up trading post of Nikaia.

1st century AD Cemenelum (Cimiez) is capital of the Roman province of Alpes Maritimae.

410 Honorat founds monastery on Lérina island (Ile Saint-Honorat).

972 Guillaume the Liberator expels Saracens from Provence.

1144 Nice becomes a Consulat, ruled by four elected Consuls.

1297 François Grimaldi takes control of Monaco.

1382 War between supporters of Charles III of Duras and Louis of Anjou.

1388 Nice forms alliance with dukes of Savoy.

1481 Cannes (but not Nice or Monaco) becomes part of France.

1538 Treaty of Nice between François I and Emperor Charles V.

1543 Siege of Nice by French and Turkish armies.

1706 Louis XIV razes Nice's citadel.

1792 French Revolutionary troops take Nice.

1822 Promenade des Anglais constructed.

1834 Lord Henry Brougham 'discovers' Cannes.

1860 Nice joins France after referendum.

1863 Casino opens in Monte Carlo.

1922 First 'Train Bleu' from Calais to the Côte d'Azur.

1931 Hotels in Cannes open in summer for the first time.

1942–3 Nice occupied by Italians.

1944 Liberation of Provence.

1946 First Cannes Film Festival.

2005 Death of Rainier III; Albert II crowned sovereign prince of Monaco.

2007 Opening of Nice tramway.

2008 Christian Estrosi elected mayor of Nice (re-elected in 2014).

2014 Princess Charlene of Monaco gives birth to twins.

2016 Bastille Day terrorist attack in Nice kills 86 and injures hundreds.

2018 A grassroots citizens' protest movement, the *gilets jaunes*, emerges fighting against the tax increase on diesel and petrol and has grown into an anti-government and anti-austerity movement.

2019 Nice, one of nine French cities, hosts the 8th FIFA Women's World Cup.

Brightly coloured houses line the streets of Monaco

WHERE TO GO

The cities of Nice, Cannes and Monte Carlo dominate one of the most celebrated stretches of coastline in the world, a 50km (30-mile) strip where heavily built-up resorts are interspersed by exclusive peninsulas, home to the happy few, and bordered on the interior by the *arrière-pays* of medieval hill villages and Alpine foothills. If you're not jet-setting by yacht or helicopter between the three, they are well connected by railway, by the A8 *autoroute* and the coastal roads, notably the spectacular trio of corniches between Nice and the Italian frontier, with hairpin bends and stunning sea views.

NICE

With a splendid position curving along the broad sweep of the Baie des Anges, **Nice** ❶ merits its reputation as the Queen of the Riviera or its affectionate Nissart name, Nissa la Bella. Central Nice divides neatly into two parts: Italianate Vieux Nice, beneath the Colline du Château, to the east of the River Paillon; and the elegant New Town, which grew up in the 19th and early 20th centuries behind the promenade des Anglais to the west. Beyond, Nice extends over a series of hills – Cimiez, Les Baumettes, Piol, Fabron – where urbanisation has largely taken over olive groves and villa gardens.

Note that all municipal museums in Nice are no longer free (as of 2015); their entrance fee is now €10 but there is also a pass which will save you money if visiting more than two museums (see page 120).

The imposing facade of the Opéra de Nice

VIEUX NICE

Against a backdrop of colourful houses, Baroque churches and campaniles, the picturesque Old Town mixes Nice at its most traditional, where some elderly residents still speak Nissart (an Occitan language related to Provençal) and restaurants serve local specialities that appear not to have changed for generations, alongside bohemian bars, art galleries and clothes shops reflecting the young cosmopolitan set that has rejuvenated the district.

Enter **Vieux Nice** on rue St-François-de-Paule, reached from place Masséna or the Jardin Albert I, passing the town hall, the chic Hôtel Beau Rivage (where Matisse stayed on his first visit in 1917) and the elaborate pink-columned facade of the **Opéra de Nice** Ⓐ (www.opera-nice.org), rebuilt in 1884 on the site of the earlier opera house, gutted when the stage curtain caught fire. Across the street, family-run Maison Auer (see page 87) has been producing candied fruits and chocolates since 1820, while Alziari (see page 87) draws connoisseurs for its olive oil, produced at its own mill in the west of the city and sold in decorative tins.

Cours Saleya

The street leads into broad **cours Saleya B** and the colourful flower market (Tue–Sun 6am–5.30pm) and fruit and vegetable market (Tue–Sun 6am–1.30pm), held under bright striped awnings, where laden stalls reflect the profusion of Riviera produce. Along with the tourists, the market is still frequented by local residents and the town's best chefs.

The market spreads into adjoining place Pierre Gautier, where you'll find many stalls run by local producers, selling nothing but lemons or delicate orange courgette flowers. On Monday, the fruit and vegetables are replaced by antiques and bric-a-brac stalls. On one side, the **Forum d'Urbanisme et d'Architecture de la Ville de Nice C** (Mon–Fri 1–5pm; free) holds interesting exhibitions about Nice's architectural heritage and urban projects. At the back of the square, the colonnaded former Palace of the Kings of Sardinia was built by the King of Piedmont when Nice was returned to Sardinia after the Revolution, and now serves as the Préfecture of the Alpes-Maritimes. Next door, the white stone Palais de Justice opens onto place du Palais, facing the russet-coloured **Palazzo Rusca D**, a Baroque mansion with impressive triple-storey arcades on one side and an 18th-century clock tower on the other. There is a second-hand book market on the square on the first and third Saturday of each month.

Cours Saleya is bordered on the sea side by **Les Ponchettes**, a double alley of low fishermen's cottages, with archways leading through to quai des Etats-Unis. Amid restaurants and a couple of exclusive shops, two vaulted halls play host to municipal exhibitions of contemporary art: **Galerie des Ponchettes** and

Galerie de la Marine (both Tue–Sun 10am–6pm, mid-Oct–mid-June from 11am). About halfway along cours Saleya, the **Chapelle de la Miséricorde** Ⓔ (temporarily closed for renovation; free) is generally considered the finest of all Nice's Baroque interiors. It belongs to the *pénitents noirs*, one of the religious lay fraternities that still thrives in the town, but is only open for extremely limited hours. Further along, on the corner with rue de la Poissonnerie, is the **Adam and Eve house**, one of the oldest buildings in the city, decorated with a Naïve 16th-century relief of Adam and Eve in the Garden of Eden.

Heart of the Old Town

However, it is in the grid of narrow, shady streets behind cours Saleya where you get a real feel for the atmosphere of Vieux Nice. Although the population started moving down from the Colline du Château in the 13th century, the town was almost entirely reconstructed in the 17th and 18th centuries, giving it much the appearance it has today: for the most part tall, simple facades in tones of yellow and orange, punctuated by Baroque churches and the occasional fine carved doorway.

In the heart of Vieux Nice, lively **place Rossetti** has a dual appeal: the ice creams and sorbets of Fenocchio (www.fenocchio.fr), where more than 90 flavours range from classic coffee and pistachio to rose, jasmine and even poppy; and the sculpted facade of **Cathédrale Sainte-Réparate** Ⓕ (Tue–Fri 9am–noon, 2–6pm, Sat until 7.30pm, Sun 9am–1pm, 3–6pm; free; http://cathedrale-nice.fr), built on a cruciform plan in the 1650s. It is dedicated to early Christian martyr Saint Reparata, the city's patron saint, whose body, accompanied by two angels (hence the name Baie des Anges) is said to have arrived here by boat after drifting across the Mediterranean from Palestine, where she had been decapitated at the age of

15. Despite its impressive painted dome over the transept and numerous Baroque side chapels, the Niçois prefer the cheer-ful little **Eglise Sainte-Rita** G (www.sainte-rita.net; Mon–Sat 7am–noon, 2.30–6pm, Sun 8am–noon, 3–6pm; free) on rue de la Poissonnerie, an intimate gem, with a skylit half-dome and profusion of sculpted saints, barley-sugar columns and sun-bursts. Take a look also at the arcaded Loggia Communale, dating from 1574, around the corner on rue de la Préfecture.

From here, rue Droite, once the main thoroughfare, leads to the Eglise Saint-Jacques-le-Majeur or **Eglise du Gésu** H (Tue 3–7pm, Thu 3–5.30pm, Sat 9am–noon, 3–6pm; free), built by the Jesuit order in 1612. It set the model for Nice's Baroque churches, with its single-naved interior full of stucco cherubs and stripy painted marble, although the blue-and-white classi-cal facade is a later reworking. Further up the street at No. 15 is the **Palais Lascaris** I (Wed–Mon 10am–6pm, mid-Oct–mid-June from 11am), the 17th-century Genoese-style mansion of the Lascaris-Ventimille family and Nice's grandest secular Baroque building. The sober street facade does not prepare you for the splendour of the interior, with its magnificent vaulted stairway, decorated with sculptures and frescoed grotesques. On the second floor, staterooms, furnished with Baroque furniture and tapestries, have spectacular painted ceilings with mythological scenes: *Venus and Adonis*, the *Abduction of Psyche* and the *Fall of Phaethon*, where youth and horses tumble from the sky amid a mass of swirling clouds. The first floor has been renovated to house the town's extensive collection of 18th- and 19th-century musical instruments.

Higher up, rue Droite runs into rue St-François and the place St-François, home to a small fish market every morning except Monday. The 17th-century former Palais Communal is now a trades union building. Further along, rue Pairolière is busy with food shops and typical Niçois bistros, while on the corner of rue Miralheti, customers queue up for plates of *socca* (see page 101) and other Niçois snacks at ever-popular Chez René Socca.

On the northern edge of Vieux Nice, the handsome **place Garibaldi ❶**, with arcaded facades and the neoclassical Chapelle du Saint-Sépulcre, was laid out in the 1780s by the King of Sardinia, Victor-Amédée, to create a monumental entry to the town on the completion of the royal carriageway from

Independence hero

Giuseppe Garibaldi, hero of Italian independence, was actually born in Nice in 1807. Although as a convinced republican he helped the French in the Franco-Prussian war of 1870, he had earlier opposed the attachment of Nice to France, which is said to be why his statue in place Garibaldi faces towards Italy.

The tram from place Garibaldi

Turin. Originally called Piazza Vittoria, it was renamed in honour of the Nice-born hero of Italian reunification whose statue stands in the middle. Note that Garibaldi is facing Italy, while beneath him two bronze women carry a baby, presumably the infant nation. Excavations during the construction of the tramway in 2007 revealed part of the antique port, aqueduct, moat and bastion. The 2,000-sq metre underground attraction is now open to the public as the **Crypte Archéologique** (entrance from Place Jacques Toja; 55-minute guided tours; no children under 7 allowed and flat shoes required; reservation obligatory, contact the Centre du Patrimoine, tel: 04 92 00 41 90 or online at www.centredupatri moinevdn.tickeasy.com).

THE COLLINE DU CHÂTEAU

Reached by assorted steep stairways from Vieux Nice, by tourist train from the quay in front of Jardin Albert I, by lift (daily Apr–Sept

The view over the Vieux Port from the Colline du Château

8.30am–8pm, Oct–Mar 8.30am–6pm; free) or by stairs at the end of quai des Etats-Unis, the **Colline du Château** Ⓚ was for centuries the heart of the medieval city that grew up around the castle, before the population moved down to the plain. Today nothing remains of the citadel, razed in 1706 on orders of Louis XIV, but the remaining mound provides a shady interlude on hot summer days, and plenty of gorgeous views over the bay. Follow the sound of water up to the cascade that tumbles dramatically over a man-made lump of rock. Below lie an amphitheatre, a café, children's playgrounds and the poorly indicated ruins of the medieval cathedral and the residential district destroyed in the siege of 1691. Slightly down the hill to the north are two graveyards: the **Jewish cemetery** with its funerary stelae, and the **Catholic cemetery** (which also includes Orthodox and Protestant tombs of some of the town's noble *émigrés*), which resembles a miniature city with gravel paths and a forest of elaborate 19th-century monuments to Niçois notables. Overlooking the sea, at the top of the lift is the solid round **Tour Bellanda**, a mock fortification reconstructed in the 19th century, where Hector Berlioz lived while composing his *King Lear Overture*. It occasionally opens to the public for exhibitions on the city's heritage.

THE VIEUX PORT

Back at sea level, quai Rauba Capéu (Nissart for 'flying hat', because of the breeze) curves around the castle mound past a striking World War I war memorial set into its cliff face, to the picturesque **Vieux Port ⓛ**. The port can also be reached from place Garibaldi along rue Ségurane, known for its cluster of antiques dealers and bric-a-brac shops. Framed by the castle hill on one side and Mont Boron on the other, the Bassin Lympia was dug out in the late 18th century (before that fishing boats were simply pulled up on the shore and Nice's main port was at nearby Villefranche-sur-Mer). At the same time, beautiful arcaded **place de l'Ile de Beauté** was built along the north side in Genoese fashion, with deep-red facades and ornate *trompe l'œil* window frames, on either side of the neoclassical sailors' church **Eglise Notre-Dame-du-Port** (Mon–Fri 9am–noon, 3–6pm, Sun 9am–noon). More tranquil than Vieux Nice, the restaurants along the eastern quay, mostly specialising in fish, are popular. Departure point for ferries to Corsica, the

Midday cannon shot

Every day at noon, a resounding boom announces the midday cannon shot fired from the Colline du Château. The tradition was inaugurated by Sir Thomas Coventry-More in the 1860s to ensure that his forgetful wife returned home in time to prepare lunch, and was perpetuated by the municipality in 1871.

port has recently been the subject of debate over controversial plans to expand it for giant cruise ships, but it has now been decided to leave it as a yachting marina and construct a new commercial port on the western side of town.

Just east of the port on boulevard Carnot, at the start of the Basse Corniche, is a curious but fascinating museum, the **Musée de Paléontologie Humaine de Terra Amata** Ⓜ (Wed–Sun 10am–6pm), situated at the bottom of an apartment block on the very spot where a tribe of elephant-hunters briefly made their settlement on the beach 400,000 years ago when the sea level was 26m (84ft) higher than today.

When the site was discovered in 1966, archaeologists worked day and night for five weeks before it was built on. The centrepiece is a large cast made of the ground, showing traces of tools, debris, animal bones and even a footprint left behind, while other exhibits include axeheads, flint tools and a reconstructed twig hut.

Beyond here wooded Mont Boron conceals luxurious residences and 11km (7 miles) of public footpaths. At the top of the hill, the 19th-century military fort is set to be transformed into an architecture centre by architect Jean Nouvel.

PROMENADE DU PAILLON

Created when the River Paillon was covered over as a hygiene measure in the 19th century, the **promenade du Paillon** marks the divide between Vieux Nice on one side and the New Town on the other. At its centre, **place Masséna** forms the symbolic heart of Nice, with elegant arcaded facades in Pompeian red, laid out in the 1840s as part of the urbanisation plan of the Consiglio d'Ornato, the council designated by King Charles-Albert in Turin to mastermind the expansion of the city. Long a traffic-clogged junction, the square was repaved and pedestrianised for the opening of the tramway in 2007, with the installation of

Elegant place Masséna

an artwork by Spanish artist Jaume Plensa, with seven resin figures atop tall metal poles, which symbolise the different continents and are illuminated in a colourful glow at night.

Towards the sea, the pleasant shady **Jardin Albert I** contains the Théâtre de Verdure, an outdoor amphitheatre used for summer concerts, and a massive bronze arc sculpture by Bernar Venet that seems to float over the lawn.

PROMENADE DES ARTS

On the other side of place Masséna, the promenade du Paillon leads to the **promenade des Arts**, created in the 1980s by mayor Jacques Médecin as part of his ambitious cultural programme. Designed by architects Yves Bayard and Henri Vidal, the Carrara marble complex comprises the Théâtre National de Nice, a terrace with sculptures by Calder, Borovsky and Niki de Saint Phalle's mosaic Loch Ness Monster fountain, and the

Ringing the changes at the MAMAC

Musée d'Art Moderne et d'Art Contemporain (MAMAC; www.mamac-nice.org; Tue–Sun 10am–6pm, mid-Oct–mid-June from 11am; guided tours in English on Sat at 4pm). The building looks rather harsh from outside but the galleries inside, where four wings are connected by glass bridges, provide a luminous setting for works from the 1960s to the present. The museum's strength lies in its collection of the Ecole de Nice, including an entire room of Yves Klein's monochromes, blue sponges and fire paintings, works by Ben, Raysse, Malaval and Christo, Arman's accumulations and cut-up musical instruments and an exceptional donation by Niki de Saint Phalle, which is complemented by parallel movements in American Pop Art, including works by Warhol, Lichtenstein and Rauschenberg.

Across the street on boulevard Risso, the **Muséum d'Histoire Naturelle** (www.mhnnice.org; Tue–Sun 10am–6pm) harks back to a decidedly different era, with stuffed birds, botanical specimens and minerals illustrating the Mediterranean habitat. In order to showcase more of its huge collection, the museum is due to relocate to a new purpose-built home in Parc Phoenix but there is no firm moving date at the time of writing.

To the north, the promenade des Arts' latest addition is heralded by the bizarre vision of the *Tête Carrée*, a massive 30m (96ft) high head by sculptor Sacha Sosno, described by the artist

⊙ THE ECOLE DE NICE

In the late 1950s and 1960s, Nice shot to the forefront of artistic creation in France, around the trio Yves Klein, Arman and Martial Raysse, championed by critic Pierre Restany, and later joined by César, Sosno, Ben, Niki de Saint Phalle and Robert Malaval. Although associated with Nouveau Réalisme (the French equivalent of Pop Art), Fluxus and Supports-Surfaces, the Ecole de Nice was more about a sense of energy and sometimes anarchist attitudes than a stylistic school. The pivotal figure was Yves Klein (1928–62), who combined painting and art actions in his famous monochromes in trademark IKB (International Klein Blue), and *anthropométries*, where female models covered in paint were rolled like a living paintbrush over the canvas. Unlike most earlier modern artists who found inspiration in the south, this was a home-grown movement: Klein, Arman and Malaval were born in Nice, César and Sosno in Marseille, Raysse at Golfe Juan. As Klein remarked in 1947: 'Even if we, the artists of Nice, are always on holiday, we are not tourists. That is the essential point. Tourists come here for the holidays; as for us, we live in this holiday land, which is what gives us our touch of madness. We amuse ourselves without thinking about religion or art or science.'

Sunbathing on a public beach

as 'an inhabited sculpture', which morphs into a cube containing the offices of the **Bibliothèque Louis Nucéra** (public library), the books and public entrance are actually underground. Beyond, before the river finally resurfaces, are the **Acropolis** congress and exhibition centres, opened in the 1980s, making Nice a major venue for international trade fairs and conferences.

THE NEW TOWN

West of the Paillon, the New Town grew up in the 19th and early 20th centuries behind the promenade des Anglais, laid out in a grid of broad avenues and garden squares roughly following the plan conceived by the Consiglio d'Ornato, planted with the exotic palms, citrus trees and bougainvillaea that have acclimatised in the south of France. After the narrow streets and deep shadows of Vieux Nice, the atmosphere here is airy and bright. Although the street plan is regular, the architecture is anything but, making this area a delight for walkers.

Promenade des Anglais

With blue chairs, white pergolas, palm trees and Belle Epoque architecture, the **promenade des Anglais** has come to symbolise the elegance of Nice – not bad for what began in 1822 as an employment exercise, when the Reverend Lewis Way opened a public subscription to construct a new footpath along the shore, linking the Old Town to the British colony that had settled on the hills further west. The promenade took on its present appearance in the 1930s when the thoroughfare was widened. Despite busy traffic, it remains a favourite place to walk, not just for the sea views but for the diversity of those who use it, from rollerbladers to elderly ladies, and for the splendour of its grand hotels, although few restaurants or boutiques line the promenade.

Running westwards from Jardin Albert I, where the Méridien Nice and neighbouring Casino Ruhl controversially replaced the old Hôtel Ruhl in the 1970s, admire the Art Deco facade of the **Palais de la Méditerranée ❻** at No. 15. Built in 1929 for American

❻ BEACHES FOR ALL

With 15 beach concessions running along the Baie des Anges, Nice's private beaches are about much more than just swimming and sunbathing, although the sun loungers *chaises longues* can be a boon on the uncomfortable pebbles. **Castel Plage** on quai des Etats-Unis at the eastern end of the Baie des Anges calls itself 'the beautiful beach for beautiful people' and likes to promote its arty image with chess matches and art exhibitions; **Beau Rivage** (www.hotelnicebeaurivage.com), belonging to the elegant Vieux Nice hotel, has a vast restaurant serving a modern Med-Asian fusion cuisine, with a DJ in the afternoons and jazz on Sundays; **Blue Beach** (www.bluebeach.fr), opposite Hôtel Negresco, is a chic place to dine by night and a child-friendly beach by day, with table tennis, a popular seawater pool for kids and water sports next door; while **Opéra Plage** is one of the oldest and most affordable beaches in Nice, with a family-friendly atmosphere and a traditional restaurant.

millionaire Frank Jay Gould, it epitomised 1930s glamour with a casino, theatre, restaurant and cocktail bar. The Palais closed in 1978 and was gutted before reopening with a modern hotel, apartments and casino behind the listed facade. At No. 27, the pink stucco Westminster still has its grandiose reception rooms, while Hôtel West End (No. 31) was the first of the promenade's grand hotels, opened in 1855.

Next door, set back from the promenade at the rear of a luscious garden laid out by Edouard André, the **Musée d'Art et d'Histoire Palais Masséna** ⓟ (Wed–Mon 10am–6pm, mid-Oct–mid-June from 11am), built in 1898 for Prince Victor Masséna, grandson of one of Napoleon's generals, has been renovated as a museum devoted to the Belle Epoque past. On the ground floor are grandiose reception rooms, with Empire furniture, sumptuous inlaid panelling and a full-length portrait of Napoleon. Upstairs, the aristocrats, artists and intellectuals who shaped 19th-century Nice are portrayed in an eclectic array of portraits, paintings, documents and memorabilia, including the cloak worn by Josephine when Napoleon was crowned King of Naples, and paintings of Old Nice. Among curiosities are a poster, in French and Italian, calling citizens to vote in the referendum for Nice to rejoin France in April 1860.

On the other side, Nice's grandest hotel, the **Hôtel Negresco** ⓠ, is an institution with its pink-and-green cupola and uniformed doormen. Designed by Edouard Niermans, with a glazed *verrière* by Gustave Eiffel over the salon, it was one of the most modern hotels in the world when it opened in 1913, with lavish bathrooms and telephones in the rooms; but with the outbreak of war in 1914 it was transformed into a hospital and Romanian owner Henri Negresco was ruined. Still a favourite with politicians and film stars, the hotel is endearingly idiosyncratic, with antique furniture, carousel horses and a kitsch souvenir shop.

Across the New Town

Parallel to the promenade des Anglais, broad **avenue Victor Hugo** is a panorama of New Town architecture, from classical villas with wrought-iron balconies and a neo-Gothic church to carved friezes, ornate Belle Epoque rotundas, Art Deco mansion blocks and streamlined 1950s zigzags. Between here and the station is the quieter **Musicians' Quarter**, with streets named after composers and the cir-

The opulent Hôtel Negresco is a Nice institution

cular Escurial Art Deco apartment block. On the eastward continuation of avenue Victor Hugo, the **Théâtre de la Photographie et de l'Image ®** (27 boulevard Debouchage; www.tpi-nice.org; Tue–Sun 10am–6pm, mid-Oct–mid-June from 11am) stages excellent photographic exhibitions. The building itself is worth a look, with a decorative theatre and neo-Renaissance ceilings.

Just off place Masséna, the **Carré d'Or**, formed by avenues de Suède and Verdun, rue Masséna and rue Paradis (and its extension, rue Alphonse Karr), is home to Nice's smartest clothes shops. Pedestrianised rue Masséna and adjoining rue de France form an animated hub with chain stores and pizzerias.

Avenue Jean-Médecin, the tree-lined shopping street that runs north from Masséna towards the station, has slid downmarket since it was laid out on the Haussmannian model with department stores, banks and opulent cafés. However, since the street has recently been pedestrianised it may now rediscover its aura of old.

WESTERN NICE

On the Beaumettes hill, the **Musée des Beaux-Arts de Nice** (33 avenue des Baumettes; www.musee-beaux-arts-nice.org; Tue–Sun 10am–6pm, mid-Oct–mid-June from 11am) occupies an extravagant mansion built in 1878 for the Ukrainian Princess Elisabeth Kotschoubey, which gives some idea of the grandeur in which the foreign aristocracy lived. Downstairs, the Old Masters section ranges from medieval religious panel paintings to 18th-century canvases by Natoire and Van Loo. Look out for two highly detailed allegorical landscapes of Water and Earth by 'Velvet' Brueghel, swarming with fantastical animals and birds, and a bravura fantasy portrait by Fragonard. At the top of the stairs, past plaster studies by Carpeaux, the 19th- and 20th-century collections include romantic pastels by Jules Chéret, best-known as a decorator and poster artist, Symbolist paintings by Gustave-Adolphe Mossa, the museum's first curator, Impressionist works by Monet and Sisley, striking portraits by Kees van Dongen, a room of cheerful seaside scenes by Raoul Dufy, and numerous paintings by Russian artist and diarist Marie Bashkirtseff. The Baumettes hill itself is worth a wander for the villas erected by British and Russian aristocrats, including the pink mock-medieval **Château des Ollières** and the **Château de la Tour**.

Further west, in a villa owned by perfumier François

Bank heist

France's biggest ever bank heist took place at the Société Générale on avenue Jean-Médecin in 1976, when Albert Spaggiari climbed through the sewers and tunnelled into the vault, leaving with 50 million francs (about 24 million euros). Arrested months later, he escaped from police custody to South America, publishing his autobiography and fraternising with Ronnie Biggs.

The Musée des Beaux-Arts' grandiose exterior

Coty in the 1920s, is the **Musée International d'Art Naïf Anatole Jakovsky** (avenue de Fabron; Wed–Mon 10am–6pm, mid-Oct–mid-June from 11am), centred around a vast collection of Naïve art donated by the Romanian art critic Anatole Jakovsky, one of the first, along with artist Jean Dubuffet, to admire the colourful meticulous works by these self-taught artists. The collection includes a portrait by Le Douanier Rousseau, obsessively detailed paintings of Paris monuments by Louis Vivin, and other major Naïve artists including Jules Lefranc, Séraphine, Rimbert, Bombois, as well as the American Grandma Moses.

Parc Floral Phoenix

At the very westernmost end of the promenade des Anglais, just before the airport and the modern Arenas business district, the **Parc Floral Phoenix** (daily Apr–Sept 9.30am–7.30pm, Oct–Mar 9.30am–6pm) is an imaginative modern botanical garden that is enjoyable for families and plant-lovers. Around the garden you'll find streams with stepping stones, aviaries with cranes, parrots and birds of prey, prairie dogs, an otter pool and crested porcupines. The vast polygonal, 25m (82ft) -high glasshouse – one of the largest in Europe – is a hothouse wonderland, where different zones recreate different tropical and desert climates, with magnificent palms, tree ferns and orchids, and habitats populated by giant iguanas and flamingos, as well as an aquarium and tanks of tarantulas. Sitting in the lake by the entrance to the park is the **Musée des Arts Asiatiques** (Wed–Mon 10am–5pm, July–Aug until 6pm; www.arts-asiatiques.com; free), a striking geometrical building symbolising Earth and Sky, designed by Japanese architect Kenzo Tange. The small but high-quality collection of art from China, Japan, India and Cambodia includes ornate samurai swords and ancient Chinese bronzes and terracottas. There is an adjoining teahouse, where the Japanese tea ceremony is performed on certain weekends.

NORTH OF THE STATION

The arrival of the railway from Paris in 1864 hastened Nice's rise as a destination for Europe's aristocracy, with a station in Louis XIII-style brick and stone facings in a new district north of the centre – what is now a typical station hinterland of cheap hotels and ethnic eateries. To the west across boulevard Gambetta, in what was once the heart of the Russian district, the newly restored **Cathédrale Orthodoxe Russe Saint-Nicolas** (boulevard Tzarewitch; daily 9am–6pm), with five onion domes and glazed tiles, is a surreal apparition amid the modern apartment blocks. Inspired by St Basil's in Moscow and inaugurated in 1912, the largest Russian Orthodox church outside Russia – and single most visited sight in Nice – was commissioned by the

Tsarina Maria Feodorovna, mother of Tsar Nicolas II, when an earlier church on rue Longchamp became too small for the growing Russian community. The atmospheric interior, laden with icons, carvings and frescoes, contains a magnificent gilded repoussé copper iconostasis (the screen that separates the congregation from the sanctuary reserved for the clergy). In the grounds is a small chapel (Wed 2.30–6pm) built on the spot where Grand Duke Nicolas Alexandrovich, son of Alexander II, died in 1865 aged 21. Nearby on avenue Paul Arène, you can also spot the 1902 Hôtel du Parc Impérial, which was originally destined for Russian families wintering in the town but became a lycée after World War I.

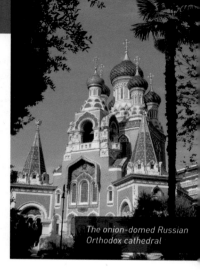

The onion-domed Russian Orthodox cathedral

On avenue Bourriglione, the extraordinary **Eglise Jeanne d'Arc** (daily 9am–6pm) is exotic in a different way. An architectural one-off, the avant-garde white concrete church designed in the 1930s by Jacques Droz resembles a box of eggs with its cluster of ovoid domes. The parabolic interior is decorated with murals by Eugène Klementieff and stylised concrete sculptures of Joan of Arc and the Crucifixion by Carlo Sarrabezolles, a pioneer in sculpting directly into wet concrete. Further north, in a 17th-century Italianate villa, largely disguised by a radical raw concrete and pebble extension, the **Villa Arson, Centre National d'Art Contemporain** (20 avenue Stéphen Liégeard; www.villa-arson.

Enjoying a leisurely game of pétanque in Cimiez

org; Wed–Mon 2–6pm, July–Aug until 7pm; free) is home to one of France's most adventurous art schools and exhibition centres.

CIMIEZ

Smart residential Cimiez is where Nice feels closest to its Belle Epoque spirit. Northeast of the centre by boulevard Carabacel and boulevard de Cimiez, this is a district of winding streets that meander uphill, lined with stucco villas amid lush gardens and palm trees. On avenue Docteur Ménard is the **Musée National Marc Chagall** Ⓢ (www.musee-chagall.fr; Wed–Mon May–Oct 10am–6pm, Nov–Apr until 5pm), where paintings by Chagall are set off by the beautifully designed low modern building and surrounding Mediterranean garden. Inaugurated in 1973, it was the first time a national museum in France had been devoted to a living artist.

It was created for his series of 17 scenes from the Old Testament, which reveal Chagall's unique ability to combine colour and narrative with a personal iconography. In another room are five rose-tinted paintings of the canticles dedicated to 'Vava', his wife Valentina Brodsky, and in the auditorium are three intense stained-glass windows and related studies depicting *The Creation of the World*.

Almost across the street, on boulevard de Cimiez, the fine Belle Epoque **Villa Paradiso** now belongs to the town's education service, but is surrounded by pretty public gardens. Further up the boulevard you can spot the White Palace and the Alhambra (distinguished by its two mosque-like minarets), grand former hotels built in the days before sea bathing became popular, when this was the most fashionable part of town to stay.

At the top of the boulevard de Cimiez, the ornate **Hôtel Excelsior Régina**, by architect Biasini, was built in 1896 in anticipation of a visit by Queen Victoria. The queen in fact stayed here twice, occupying the entire west wing with a suite of more than 70 rooms, an event commemorated in the crown over the entrance and a marble statue outside. Converted into apartments in the 1930s, this is where Matisse lived at the end of his life, sketching on the ceiling from his bed with a brush attached to a long pole.

Roman Remains

Across the street are the scant remains (entrance tunnels, a few tiers of seats) of the **Roman amphitheatre**, which once seated 5,000 people and is now used for the Nice Jazz Festival each summer (see page 90). To get a clearer idea of Nice's Roman incarnation as the city of Cemenelum, visit the adjacent **Musée Archéologique** (Wed–Mon 10am–6pm), which has displays of statues, glassware and jewellery excavated in the area and, in the basement, sarcophagi and inscribed stelae from a nearby necropolis, as well as the chance to try out some Roman board games.

The most interesting part of the museum is the archaeological site outside, where extensive remains include some imposing walls and canals and pieces of hypocaust (the underfloor heating system) from three bathing complexes dating from Cemenelum's 3rd-century heyday, as well as a 5th-century palaeo-Christian baptistery.

Homage to Matisse

Behind the ruins, you can spot the rust-coloured Genoese villa that houses the **Musée Matisse** ❶ (164 avenue des Arènes; www.musee-matisse-nice.org; Wed–Mon 10am–6pm, Nov–Apr until 5pm), though the entrance is around the corner, reached through a grove of ancient olive trees. The extensive collection hung around the house and in the discreet underground modern extension spans the artist's entire career from early paintings of the 1890s to his late paper cut-outs, allowing one to see how he assimilated such inspirations as Riviera sunlight, patterned textiles, classical sculpture and voyages to North Africa and Tahiti.

Highlights include Fauve portraits, the vibrant *Still Life with Grenadines*, small oil studies for different versions of *La Danse, Odalesque au Coffret Rouge*, a series of small bronze heads of *Jeannette*, and the colourful late cut-out *Flowers and Fruit*, made in 1953.

Pay further homage to Matisse in the simple slab-like tomb that sits on its own terrace in the gardens

Nice Observatory

Charles Garnier and Gustave Eiffel, two of the 19th century's greatest architects and engineers, collaborated in the construction of the Nice Observatory on Mont Gros, east of the city above the Saint-Roch district. Still at the cutting edge of research, it is open for guided visits (www.oca.eu; Wed, Sat 2.45pm).

The rust-coloured facade of the Musée Matisse

of the **Cimiez Cemetery** just up the road, the burial place for many British and Russian aristocrats. Painter Raoul Dufy is also buried here, although on the other side of the cemetery. You can admire fine views of the hills of Nice and down to the coast from the adjoining rose garden before visiting the **Eglise Franciscaine** (Mon–Sat 10am–noon, 3–5.30pm; free). Although the church facade has been rebuilt in a rather garish style, the interior is a simple Gothic structure with walls and vaults entirely covered in murals, and a Baroque retable. The church contains three paintings by local master Ludovico Bréa (see page 19): a *Pièta* triptych from around 1475, a *Crucifixion* of 1512 and a late *Deposition* attributed to Bréa, dating from around 1520. It is interesting to contrast the Gothic emotion depicted in the early angular *Pièta* with the luminosity and symmetrical layout of the later *Crucifixion*, with its solidly posed figures and perspective that carries to a far-off landscape.

Taking it easy on La Croisette

Upstairs, the monastic buildings contain a small museum presenting the history of the Franciscan order in Nice, through paintings, manuscripts, a reconstituted monk's cell and a small, simple chapel.

CANNES

Cannes ❷ is the glamour capital of the Alpes-Maritimes, a place for hedonists to succumb to the indulgence of sun, sand, shopping and more shopping. Yet unlike many Riviera resorts, it does qualify as a real town with an all-year population where, alongside some of the glitziest shops in the world, the Old Town still has the allure of a Provençal village, and men play *boules* under the trees in front of the town hall.

By far the most scenic way to arrive in Cannes is from the west along the Corniche de l'Estérel, although traffic is often nose to tail during the holiday season. If you are approaching from the *autoroute*, the road descends to the coast from Le Cannet by boulevard Carnot, past modern apartment blocks and some fine Belle Epoque buildings, including the Palais de Justice and the Hôtel Cavendish, to arrive at the Palais des Festivals.

Sitting on the seafront between the Old Port and La Croisette, the **Palais des Festivals** Ⓐ (www.palaisdesfestivals.com) is the symbol of film festival glamour. Although the building itself is an entirely uninspiring piece of 1980s architecture, nicknamed 'the bunker', it is part of the Cannes Festival myth, as epitomised by the famous walk up *les marches* – the steps leading to the grand auditorium – and the trail of handprints made by film stars and directors in the terracotta pavement outside. With its 18 auditoria, however, the Palais is used for numerous events – music industry awards, advertising and property development fairs, luxury shopping and tourism conventions, rock concerts and chess tournaments. The building also contains the Casino Croisette, the tourist office and the Rotonde de Lérins extension overlooking the sea.

LA CROISETTE

Running east along the bay from the Palais, **La Croisette**, Cannes's palm tree-lined seafront promenade, marked the resort's social ascension in the early 20th century with a trio of legendary palace hotels: the **Majestic**, opened in 1926, the ornate **Carlton** Ⓑ, opened in 1912, with two cupolas, supposedly modelled on the breasts of celebrated courtesan La Belle Otero, and the Art Deco **Martinez** Ⓒ, built by Emmanuel Martinez, who modestly named it after himself. When it opened in 1929, just in time for the transition to the summer season, it was France's largest hotel, with 476 spacious master bedrooms and 56 for clients' personal staff.

La Croisette is still a hub of activity, animated by the parade of open-top cars and illuminated at night for an evening

The festival action unfolds at the Palais des Festivals

promenade. In summer, the long sandy beach is almost entirely taken up by private beach concessions, with restaurants, deck-chairs and jetties for parascending and water-skiing, although there is a small, crowded and fuel-fume-polluted public section between the Majestic jetty and the Palais des Festivals.

The first section of La Croisette is home to the smartest designer labels and jewellers, fun for window-shopping even if you're not in the market for evening gowns and diamond tiaras. Set amid lawns halfway along at No. 47, dwarfed by many of its neighbours, **La Malmaison** Ⓓ (Mon–Fri 9am–5pm) is the last Belle Epoque remnant of the Grand Hôtel, staging a mixed bag of art exhibitions.

Further along, the villas have largely been replaced by apartment buildings, with sun-catching balconies. At the east end, beyond pine-shaded gardens and the Port Canto yachting marina, La Croisette terminates at the Pointe de la Croisette promontory, where the **Palm Beach Casino**, built in 1929 and reopened in 2002 after several years' closure, contains a restaurant, gaming rooms, nightclub and an outdoor casino in summer.

Running parallel to La Croisette, **rue d'Antibes**, which follows the trace of the old royal road between Toulon and Antibes,

⊙ CANNES FILM FESTIVAL

For 10 days in May, Cannes becomes capital of world cinema. Couturiers lend actresses their most extravagant creations, paparazzi snap cast and directors climbing *les marches* of the Palais des Festivals, fans press behind the barriers in hope of a signature, 4,000 journalists try to get slots in the interview room and Paris's trendiest nightclubs decamp south. Launched in the 1930s, when the Venice Film Festival was tainted by Fascism, Cannes was chosen for its sunny location and its promise to build a special auditorium. In the event, war broke out and the first festival was held in 1946 in the municipal casino. Over the years, the festival has spawned the International Critics' Week and Directors' Fortnight, as well as the vast film market dealings that go on around the port. Although a strictly professional event, the organisers have made some concessions to the public with the Cinéma de la Plage open-air screenings.

The festival sticks determinedly to its art-movie reputation. Directors like Ken Loach and the Belgian Dardenne brothers are regulars; big-budget Hollywood blockbusters tend to be screened out of competition, and the selection remains wildly international – films from Mexico, Iran and Romania all get a look in. There are occasionally some heartwarming surprises – in 2008 the Palme d'Or went to Laurent Cantet's *The Class*, acted by a cast of Paris schoolkids (www.festival-cannes.com).

is almost entirely devoted to the art of shopping, where mainstream fashion chains mix with more cutting-edge stores. Amid the storefronts, if you look up, is some fine late 19th-century architecture, with sculptures and wrought-iron decoration. At night, the block formed by rue des Frères Pradignac, rue du Commandant-André and rue du Dr Gérard-Monod is a focus for nightlife, with its restaurants and lounge bars.

THE PORT VIEUX AND MARCHÉ FORVILLE

West of the Palais des Festivals is the **Port Vieux**, reconstructed in the 19th century to meet the demands of its new British visitors. Today, a few surviving fishing boats sit somewhat incongruously among the luxury yachts, surrounded by the colour-washed facades of the quai St-Pierre and brasseries, bars and shellfish restaurants of avenue Félix Faure. Next to the pompous 19th-century town hall, the plane tree-lined **Allées de la Liberté** contain a vintage bandstand, *pétanque* pitches and a flower market. In the adjoining square, on a plinth above a very British-looking lion is a statue of Lord Henry Brougham, credited with discovering Cannes for the British after spending a night here in 1834. Nearby, rue du Bivouac Napoléon recalls another visitor, who camped here after landing at Golfe-Juan on 1 March 1815, when he escaped from exile on Elba.

Behind the port, pedestrianised rue Meynadier is lined with inexpensive clothes and shoe stores at one end, simple restaurants, bars and food shops at the other, while a street back, **Marché Forville** ❺ (Tue–Sun 7am–1pm) covered market provides a taste of the 'real Cannes' – though you have to arrive early to find what's left of the local catch: sardines, tiny sea bream and little rockfish. In summer, stalls are a tempting feast of tomatoes, courgettes, small aubergines, hot little red peppers, melons, peaches and green figs.

LE SUQUET

Before the arrival of the British in the 19th century, Le Suquet was pretty much all there was of Cannes: a few picturesque streets and stepped alleyways of tall yellow-and-pink houses winding up the hill around the fortress constructed by the monks of Lérins. Quiet and villagey by day, Le Suquet is particularly lively at night, when visitors flock to the bars and restaurants on rue St-Antoine and its

Steep side street in Le Suquet

continuation, rue du Suquet. At the top, beyond the 16th-century church of **Notre-Dame de l'Espérance**, whose parvis is used for open-air concerts in summer, shady place de la Castre offers a fine view from the ramparts. Entered through a pretty garden, the cool, whitewashed rooms of the former castle now contain the **Musée de la Castre** 🇫 (July–Aug daily 10am–7pm, Apr–June, Sept Tue–Sun 10am–1pm, 2–6pm, Oct–Mar Tue–Sun 10am–1pm, 2–5pm), a surprising ethnographic collection donated by the Dutch Baron Lycklama in 1877. An eclectic array of masks, headdresses, statues and ceremonial daggers from Tibet, Nepal and Ladakh, bone carvings from Alaska, animal-shaped jugs from Latin America and archaeological finds from ancient Egypt, Cyprus and Mesopotamia are complemented by a couple of rooms of paintings by Orientalist and Provençal painters. From the court-yard you can climb 109 narrow steps up the 11th-century **Tour du Suquet** for panoramic views over the town, port and bay.

An ethereal mural in Le Cannet

LA CROIX DES GARDES

West of the port, the **Plage du Midi**, with the railway running along the side, is less chic than La Croisette, but its largely public beach makes it a better bet if you're not going to one of the private establishments. Back on the other side of the railway, **La Croix des Gardes** district is where many British settlers built their residences in a variety of styles ranging from Palladian villas to rustic cottages and crenellated castles, following on from Lord Brougham, whose neoclassical Villa Eléonore stands on avenue du Docteur-Picaud. Most are now private apartments only glimpsed from the road amid luxuriant gardens, but you can see the **Château de la Tour** on avenue Font de Veyre (now a hotel, see page 139) and the **Villa Rothschild** (1 avenue Jean de Noailles), built in 1881 for the Baronne de Rothschild, and now the municipal library, whose gardens planted with palms, catalpas and other exotic species have become a pleasant public park. At the top of the hill, boulevard Leader and avenue de Noailles emerge in a surprisingly wild protected nature area, crossed by several footpaths, and marked at the top by a glistening steel cross.

Prosper Mérimée (1803–70), novelist and inspector of historic monuments, was another winter visitor, staying with English sisters Emma and Fanny Lagdon. He preferred Cannes to Nice, which he thought as crowded as Paris, but detested many of the new buildings (see box). He is buried alongside many British settlers, including Lord Brougham, and numerous Russian aristocrats and artists, in the **Cimetière du Grand Jas**, which descends in scenic terraces down the eastern flank of the hill.

LE CANNET

Reached up boulevard Carnot, on the hill above Cannes, the suburb of Le Cannet was originally settled by Italian immigrants brought here by the monks of Lérins in the 16th century to cultivate the olive groves. The old centre, focused on rue St-Sauveur and place Bellevue, still has the air of a little Provençal hill village with narrow streets and a belfry with a wrought-iron campanile. Le Cannet is particularly associated with painter Pierre Bonnard, who bought a house here in 1926; staying largely remote from the social whirl of the coast below, he painted the village rooftops, the view from his window,

Mérimée's verdict

'The English who have built here deserve to be impaled for the architecture they have brought into this beautiful country. You cannot imagine how distressed I am to see these stage-set castles posed on these lovely hills.'

with patches of yellow mimosa, or his beloved wife Marthe. Next to the town hall the Hôtel Saint-Vianney has been turned into the **Musée Bonnard** (www.museebonnard.fr; July–Aug Tue–Wed and Fri–Sun 10am–8pm, Thu until 9pm, Sept–June Tue–Sun 10am–6pm).

LA CALIFORNIE

Later arrivals often built their villas on the hills of La Californie and Super-Cannes on the eastern side of town, still the most exclusive area to live, though fences and security gates mean that few are visible from the street. Two that can be visited are the **Chapelle Bellini** (Parc Fiorentina, 67 bis avenue de Vallauris; Mon–Fri 2–5pm; free), an Italianate chapel built in 1884 that was more recently the studio of painter Emmanuel Bellini, and the **Villa Domergue** (15 avenue Fiesole; July–Sept daily 11am–7pm), the house and terraced Tuscan-style gardens designed in 1934 by society portrait painter Jean-Gabriel Domergue. After a successful career as a graphic artist for the fashion houses, Domergue, who had been taught by Toulouse-Lautrec and Degas, moved south in the 1920s, where he organised big parties, designed posters and churned out countless languid portraits of women, including Brigitte Bardot and Nadine de Rothschild. There are paintings and sculptures by Domergue and his wife around the house and garden, and the villa is used for temporary exhibitions and outdoor jazz concerts in summer. Lower down towards the sea, the neo-Gothic **Eglise Saint-Georges** (27 avenue Roi Albert) was built in 1887 in memory of Queen Victoria's youngest son, Prince Leopold, who died here in 1884. This was also the area favoured by the Russian aristocracy, as witnessed by the starry blue onion dome of the **Eglise Orthodoxe Russe Saint-Michel-Archange** (impasse des Deux-Eglises, 40 boulevard Alexandre III).

The nature reserve on Ile Sainte-Marguerite

THE ILES DE LÉRINS

A 10-minute boat ride from the Port Vieux, the **Iles de Lérins** G seem a world apart from La Croisette: yet for much of its history the little fishing settlement of Cannes was merely a dependence of the monastery on Ile Saint-Honorat and the islands were frequently a prized trophy in European wars.

Ile Sainte-Marguerite

The larger of the two islands, **Sainte-Marguerite** is perfect for walks and picnics, and despite numerous ferries a day in summer it's still possible to get away from the crowds. There's a sheltered beach to the west of the harbour, and plenty of smaller rocky creeks to be found along the 8km (5-mile) footpath that circles the island. En route are great views of the Estérel mountain range, Ile Saint-Honorat and the Bay of Cannes. Most of the interior is covered in forest – eucalyptus, holm-oak, aleppo and parasol

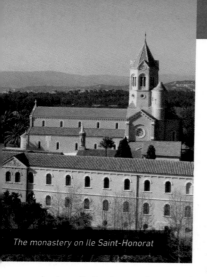

The monastery on Ile Saint-Honorat

pines – and traversed by numerous footpaths and picnic sites. A botanical trail points out the most interesting plants, while the **Etang du Batéguier**, a small brackish lake near the western tip, is a nature reserve drawing a wide variety of birds. Look out also for a couple of *fours à boulets* – stoves used to heat up cannon balls.

Dominating the cliff on the north side of the island, a short uphill walk from the harbour is the impressive star-shaped, bastioned **Royal Fort**. It was begun by Cardinal Richelieu, continued by the Spanish who occupied the island from 1635–7 during the Thirty Years War, when it made a convenient point on the way between Spain and Italy, and given its final form by Louis XIV's brilliant military engineer Vauban. Assorted buildings within the ramparts contain the long gunpowder store, the barracks and a chapel.

The old keep, which was erected in the 17th century around a medieval tower, contains the **Musée de la Mer** (June–Sept daily 10am–5.45pm, Oct–Mar Tue–Sun 10.30am–1.15pm, 2.15–4.45pm, Apr–May until 5.45pm), which reveals several different eras of the defence of the island. Vaulted Roman cisterns, constructed to store precious water, now contain a maquette of the original Roman *castrum*, along with fragments of mosaic and a collection of Greek amphorae found from shipwrecks that testify to an ancient wine trade. In the late 17th century, after the Revocation of the Edict of Nantes, it became one of four royal prisons in the Mediterranean where Protestants and others seen to pose a threat to the crown were held without trial. The cells contain a memorial to six Protestant priests held here, as well as a manuscript written by Scottish prisoner Andrew MacDonald, found in a hole in the wall. The room that most stirs the imagination, however, is the cell of the Man in the Iron Mask, where the mysterious figure immortalised by Alexandre Dumas was imprisoned from 1687–98.

Ile Saint-Honorat

Smaller and wilder than Ile Sainte-Marguerite, Ile Saint-Honorat was for centuries one of the most important religious sites in Europe, home to the powerful monastery founded around 410 by Honoratus and a small group of companions, becoming an important place of pilgrimage. On a flat spit of land jutting out at the southern tip of the island is the severe **Monastère-Donjon**, which was fortified against pirate raids, with chapels and refectories set around an unusual two-tiered cloister. The remains of seven ancient chapels are dotted around the island, including the 10th-century Chapelle de la Trinité and the unusual octagonal Chapelle Saint-Caprien. During the

Getting there

Several companies run trips from Cannes to the islands all year round, leaving from quai Laubeuf beyond the car park at the western end of the port, but note that you cannot combine both islands in one trip. Boats to Sainte-Marguerite: Horizon, tel: 04 92 98 71 36, www.horizon-lerins.com; Trans Côte d'Azur, tel: 04 92 98 71 30, www.trans-cote-azur.com; to Saint-Honorat: Planaria, tel: 04 92 98 71 38, www.cannes-ilesdelerins.com.

Revolution, the monastery was confiscated as national goods and sold off to a Parisian actress who used it to host parties. In 1859, the island was acquired by the bishop of Fréjus and a new **monastery** (www.abbayedelerins.com; daily guided thematic visits) was rebuilt around a medieval cloister, which now houses a small community of Cistercian monks who cultivate the vineyard and produce a plant-based liqueur called Lérina. Dining on the terrace of the island's only restaurant, La Tonnelle (see page 112), offers wonderful views across the coast.

MONACO

The second-smallest state in Europe – after the Vatican – is a tiny autocratic anomaly in the midst of republican France: a surreal place squeezed between sea and mountain, where princes and princesses and the paraphernalia of monarchy exist alongside skyscrapers and international banks that give it the air of a mini Hong Kong; a tax haven for tennis players; and a jet-setters' playground, where the chief pastime is driving Ferraris around the hairpin bends. The Riviera's land pressure is at its greatest here, and Belle Epoque villas are dwarfed by apartment blocks, all straining for a sea view. Monaco divides into several distinct districts: Monte Carlo around the Casino, plus its eastward beach extension Larvotto; La Condamine around the Port Hercule; Monaco-Ville, the original town up on its rock, also known as Le Rocher; Fontvieille, on reclaimed land on the western side; and Moneghetti, inland on top of the hill. It may be just 2km (1.2 miles) square, but a one-way system and lots of tunnels make navigation complicated. Leave the car in a car park and use taxis, the efficient bus service, or go by foot – a useful system of lifts and stairways helps pedestrians to negotiate the steep hills.

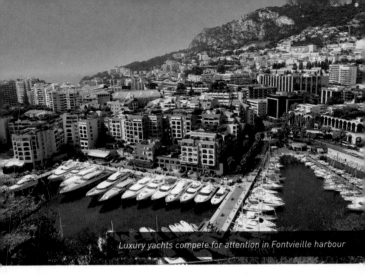

Luxury yachts compete for attention in Fontvieille harbour

MONTE CARLO

Monte Carlo ❸ is the district that for most people epitomises Monaco, centred around the hub of **place du Casino**. The neatly manicured lawns and fountains of the Jardin des Boulengrins, which descend from boulevard des Moulins, make a splendid approach to the **Casino de Monte Carlo** Ⓐ (www.montecarlosbm.com; daily 2pm–late; over 18s, ID required, smart attire; group tours 9am–1pm) with its sculptures on the facade, green copper roof and twin turrets. It is hard to imagine that this was simply an olive-tree-covered hill until the 1860s, when Prince Charles III, in search of a new source of revenue following the cession of Menton and Roquebrune to France, had the bright idea of opening a casino. After an unenthusiastic start, the prince awarded the concession to run it to François Blanc, founder of the Société des Bains de Mer de Monaco (SBM). This company (its main shareholder is now the State of

Café de Paris on place du Casino

Monaco) still runs the majority of Monte Carlo's finest hotels, restaurants, casinos, spas, sporting facilities and nightclubs.

By day, tourists crowd round to take photos; by night, this is still the most glamorous of Monaco's numerous gambling establishments, where roulette and blackjack are played against a backdrop of allegorical paintings and chandeliers. There's a separate entrance for the *salons privés*, reserved for high-staking players. In 1878, Blanc's widow Marie called in architect Charles Garnier, who had recently designed the Paris Opera, to add an opera house to encourage gamblers to stay in town a little longer. The **Salle Garnier** was inaugurated in January 1879, tacked on the back of the casino. Over the years the opera has welcomed renowned singers, from Adelina Patty, Nelly Melba and Russian Schaliapine to Plácido Domingo, as well as becoming home to Diaghilev's Ballets Russes. The auditorium is a gorgeous confection, painstakingly restored in

2005 right down to five different shades of gold leaf. Opera and casino share the same foyer, giving a unique opportunity for a flutter in the interval.

Around the Casino

On one side of the casino, historic brasserie **Café de Paris** has a superb terrace for watching the comings and goings on the square; inside, slot machines are busy all day long, while the renovated gaming tables have a Formula 1 theme. Across the square, Rolls-Royces and Ferraris line up outside the **Hôtel de Paris B**, built by the SBM in 1864, the first and still grandest of the grand hotels houses the Louis XV restaurant and the Bar Américain. In the splendid lobby, the horse's knee on the equestrian statue of Louis XIV has been polished gold by superstitious gamblers hoping for good luck.

This is also Monaco's smartest shopping territory, with jewellers and designer labels lining avenue des Beaux-Arts and place Beaumarchais between the Hôtel de Paris and the huge Belle Epoque **Hôtel Hermitage** (which now has a putting green on the roof).

Below the Casino gardens, a lift and stairs descend to the roof terraces of the huge Spélugues complex (the original name of the district before Prince Charles renamed it after himself) built in 1978. Constructed like a series of overlapping hexagons

As seen on screen

The Casino de Monte Carlo is a favourite movie location. It features in Hitchcock's *Rebecca* and his Riviera romp *To Catch a Thief*, with Grace Kelly and Cary Grant, in Jacques Demy's *La Baie des Anges* and Victor Saville's *24 Hours of a Woman's Life*. Another casino habitué is James Bond, who tries his luck in both *GoldenEye* and *Never Say Never Again*.

jutting out on concrete stilts into the water over a roaring road tunnel, it comprises the 616-room Fairmont Hotel, apartments and the **Auditorium Rainier III** congress centre, which has a mosaic on the roof by Op artist Victor Vasarely.

Further East

In a garden on avenue Princesse Grace, the peach-and-cream stucco **Villa Sauber** is one of two villas (the other is Villa Paloma in Meneghetti, see page 77) that are the home of the **Nouveau Musée National Monaco** (NMNM; www.nmnm. mc; daily 10am–6pm). The museum aims to showcase the

⊙ MONACO GRAND PRIX

Held around the narrow streets of Monte Carlo and La Condamine, the Monaco Grand Prix is considered the slowest but most difficult of the Formula 1 races, with its notorious chicane bends, changes of level and road-tunnel exit. The first race was organised on 14 April 1929 by the Automobile Club de Monaco and won by a certain William Grover-Williams in a green Bugatti, and it became part of the new Formula 1 season in the 1950s. Since then Ayrton Senna won it six times, Graham Hill and Michael Schumacher five times each. People reserve tickets for the grandstands along the Port Hercule or in race-side hotels, restaurants and apartment roof terraces months, even years, ahead, champagne lunches included, or watch from private yachts in the harbour. Once the grandstands and barriers have been dismantled, the roads are returned to the Bentleys, Ferraris and Lamborghinis that generally occupy them, though various companies offer tourists the chance of experiencing at least a semblance of the thrills in a red Ferrari.

Monaco's man-made Larvotto Beach

principality's cultural heritage in a contemporary manner and the changing exhibitions at Villa Sauber (temporarily closed at the time of writing) focus on the 'art of theatre' or set design.

Over the street, the **Jardins Japonais** Ⓒ (daily 9am–sunset; free) on the quayside provides a touch of oriental Zen calm, with streams traversed by stepping stones and Japanese bridges, Shinto shrines, raked gravel and trees trimmed into sculptural forms. Behind it, the polygonal glass-and-copper structure overlooking the sea is just the tip of the iceberg that is **Grimaldi Forum** (www.grimaldiforum.com; ticket office Tue–Sat noon–7pm): a huge, partially buried venue for art exhibitions, congresses, concerts and occasional ballet and opera productions.

Beyond here Monaco's man-made **Larvotto Beach** is mostly public, with coarse imported sand and a couple of restaurants, bordered to the east by the Méridien Beach Plaza and the

Sporting Club d'Été, opened in the 1970s, home to restaurants and Monaco's most famous nightclub, Jimmy'z.

LA CONDAMINE

The natural deep-water harbour of the **Port Hercule ⓓ** has been used ever since the Greek Phocaean trading post of Monoikos. Today the port is one of the prime spots for the Formula 1 Grand Prix, when grandstands are set up along quai Albert I. The rest of the year, with its large outdoor swimming pool (transformed into an ice rink in winter) and pizzerias, it is used for all sorts of events, ranging from international showjumping in June to a water splash and funfair in August. Quai Antoine I is home to the ever-fashionable American restaurant Stars 'n' Bars (see page 114), while the spectacle of swanky yachts with multi-storey decks and uniformed crews makes **quai des Etats-Unis** a favourite promenade. The port has grown since 2000, with the construction of a counter-jetty, designed to keep out easterly winds and welcome in the yachts of the ultra-rich, and a massive semi-floating concrete dyke towed across from Spain to accommodate vast cruise ships.

Alongside the port, now squeezed under a flyover, the **Eglise Sainte-Dévote** (daily 10am–noon, 4–6pm; free) is dedicated to the principality's patron saint, Corsican Saint Devota, who is said to have drifted ashore here in the 4th century. The church, begun in the 11th century, was almost entirely reconstructed in the 19th. A boat is burnt on the cobbled square in front each 26 January on the eve of the saint's feast.

Inland, mainly low-rise **La Condamine** is about as close as Monaco gets to everyday living, with a few Belle Epoque terraces and the lively restaurant-lined rue Princesse Caroline. Under the shadow of Le Rocher, arcaded **place d'Armes** is home to a **covered food market** (mornings daily) with quirky

Palais Princier

bars and stalls inside selling meat, patisseries and pasta – each with a photo of the current prince proudly on display – and fruit and vegetable stalls outside on the square.

MONACO-VILLE

Sitting on top of its rock, Le Rocher or Monaco-Ville is dominated by the picturebook Palais Princier on place du Palais, still the royal residence, ruled – apart from a few interludes – by the Grimaldi family ever since François Grimaldi sneaked in disguised as a monk in 1297. Walk up from place d'Armes or take one of the frequent buses, which deposit you on place de la Visitation, a 10-minute walk from place du Palais. The square lined with cannons and pyramids of cannon balls provides great views from the ramparts on each side. Each day, the changing of the guard takes place promptly at 11.55am, accompanied by much marching and drum-beating.

The **Palais Princier** Ⓔ (www.palais.mc; daily Apr–mid-Oct 10am–6pm) was constructed around the fortress begun by the Genoans in the 13th century and embellished during the Renaissance when the frescoed, arcaded Galerie d'Hercule overlooking the Cour d'Honneur was built, with a double horse-shoe staircase modelled on Fontainebleau; this inner court-yard was the venue of the wedding ceremony of Prince Albert II and Charlene Wittstock in July 2011. The excellent audio guide (complete with a welcome from the prince) included with the ticket moves through the State Apartments, taking in the mir-ror gallery, the bright-blue Louis XV room, panelled Mazarin room and the bedroom where Edward Augustus, duke of York and brother of George III, died in 1767 after falling ill en route for Genoa; and finishes in the Throne Room, with a fireplace in La Turbie marble and a canopied Empire-style throne where Prince Albert II was crowned in 2005, all accompanied by a large number of royal portraits.

Exploring the Old Town

The Old Town's handful of narrow streets of pastel-coloured houses, now largely taken up by souvenir shops, make an intriguingly folksy contrast to Monte Carlo. Bypassed by most visitors is the **Chapelle de la Miséricorde** Ⓕ (daily 10am–6pm; free) with striped marble walls, white marble sculptures and a painted wooden sculpture of the *Dead Christ* attributed to Monaco-born François-Joseph Bosio (1768–1845), which is paraded through the town on Good Friday. Also worth visiting is the pretty 17th-century **Chapelle de la Visitation** Ⓖ (Tue–Sun 10am–4pm), which provides an appropriate setting for a fine private collection of Baroque religious art that includes paint-ings of saints Peter and Paul by Rubens, works by Ribera and Zurbarán, and a set of Spanish grisaille paintings.

Cathedral and Aquarium

The **Cathédrale** (daily May–Sept 8.30am–7pm, Oct–Apr 8.30am–6pm, closed during services; free) was built in 1875 and is a severe neo-Romanesque affair, with flags along the nave and a Byzantine-style mosaic over the altar, made by the same craftsmen who worked on the Casino. In the side chapels are reliquaries of Saint Devota, Monaco's patron saint, and of Roman legionary Saint Roman, and an altarpiece by Ludovico Bréa showing St Nicolas surrounded by saints, among them Saint Devota. The simple slab-like tombs of the princes of Monaco are set into the ground around the apse, drawing visitors and pilgrims especially to those of Princess Grace, who was laid to rest in 1982, and Prince Rainier, who joined her here in 2005.

Monaco-Ville's neo-Romanesque cathedral

In an imposing white building that descends down the cliff face from avenue St-Martin, the extremely popular **Musée Océanographique et Aquarium ❶** (www.oceano. mc; daily Apr–June and Sept 10am–7pm, July–Aug 9.30am–8pm, Oct–Mar 10am–6pm) was founded in 1910 by sea-faring Prince Albert I, 'the scientist prince', who trained in the French navy before setting off on countless oceanographic expeditions, mostly to the Arctic. The upstairs museum is an elegant time-warp tribute to his voyages, with its wooden cases, whale skeletons, navigation charts, and glass jars containing preserved specimens. The chief attraction is the downstairs aquarium, where cleverly lit tanks, fed by water pumped in directly from the sea, include a shark lagoon and living coral reefs populated by brightly coloured species from the Mediterranean and tropical oceans.

In the gardens that descend below avenue de la Porte Neuve, the ruined 18th-century **Fort Saint-Antoine** on the headland is now an amphitheatre used in summer for outdoor performances, while lower down by the Parking des Pêcheurs car park is the **Cinéma d'Été**, where recently released movies are screened outdoors in the summer months.

Homage to Grace

The parcours Princesse Grace is a trail of 25 places in the principality that are associated with the former Hollywood film star Grace Kelly, who married Prince Rainier III in 1956. Sites are marked by panels with black-and-white press photos of the princess carrying out royal functions.

FONTVIEILLE

This entire new district, created on 25 hectares (60 acres) of land reclaimed from the sea, was one of the pharaonic projects of the 1960s that earned Rainier III the label 'the builder prince' – a vast complex of bland apartment blocks in neo-Provençal tones around a yachting marina, with a number of bars and brasseries popular with international expats. West of the marina bordering Cap d'Ail lie the heliport, the **Stade Louis II** (3 avenue des Castelans), home to Monaco football club, which plays in the French premier league, along with an athletics track and an Olympic-size swimming

Along the parcours Princesse Grace

pool; the Espace Châpiteau, a permanent big top used for the prestigious circus festival each January; and the **Princesse Grace rose garden** (daily 8am–sunset; free), where 4,000 rose bushes have been planted in a heart-shaped design, in memory of the princess who died under what are still mysterious circumstances in a car accident on the Corniche in 1982.

Local people, however, come to Fontvieille for the shopping centre, with a large Carrefour hypermarket. From here, escalators climb to **Terrasses de Fontvieille**, a rather bizarre setting for a cluster of small museums.

A Trio of Museums

The **Musée des Timbres et des Monnaies** (www.oetp-monaco. com; daily July–Aug 10am–6pm, Sept–June 10am–5pm), with a stamp shop on site, is devoted to Monaco stamps (since 1885) and coins (since 1641), which are popular with philatelists and numismatists. The **Musée Naval** (daily 10am–6pm) houses ship models tracing maritime history.

Not surprisingly in motor-racing-crazy Monaco, the most substantial member of the group is the **Collection de Voitures Anciennes de SAS le Prince de Monaco** ❶ (www.palais.mc; daily 10am–6pm), the collection of vintage cars amassed by Prince Rainier III. They range from a Dion Bouton made in 1903 and an early Panhard et Levassor from 1907 via lots of vintage Rolls-Royces and Princess Grace's humbler Renault Floride to modern racing cars, including Nigel Mansell's Formula 1 Ferrari, as well as some utilitarian vehicles from the Monaco fire brigade and some early horse-drawn carriages. A recent addition is a prototype racing car ALA50 manufactured in Monaco by Monte Carlo Automobile and given to Prince Albert II for his 50th birthday in 2008.

To the side of the museum is a small zoo, the **Jardin Animalier** ❷ (daily June–Sept 9am–noon, 2–7pm, Jan–Feb 10am–noon, 2–5pm, Mar–May 10am–noon, 2–6pm), founded by Prince Rainier. Among its creatures are rhesus monkeys, a hippo, pythons, a rare white tiger and exotic birds.

MONEGHETTI

Monaco's last attraction on the way out of town towards Nice is probably its best. The **Jardin Exotique** ❸ (62 boulevard du Jardin Exotique; www.jardin-exotique.mc; daily Nov–Jan 9am–5pm, Feb–Apr and Oct 9am–6pm, May–Sept 9am–7pm), opened in 1933, is a fantasy land of cacti and succulents, among them giant agaves, whole colonies of grandmother's pincushions and 11m (36ft) high euphorbes, some of them over a century old, planted in steep terraces and gulleys down the cliff. The entrance ticket also includes the **Grotte de l'Observatoire** (guided visits only) at the foot of the garden, a deep limestone cave full of stalactites and stalagmites, and the rather dry **Musée d'Anthropologie Préhistorique**, displaying archaeological finds, mainly from the Grimaldi caves just across the Italian border.

The 1920s **Villa Paloma**, perched on a hillside nearby overlooking the harbour, is one of two homes (the other is Villa Sauber, see page 68) of the Nouveau Musée National de Monaco (www.nmnm.mc). Here, the changing exhibitions all have the theme of 'art and

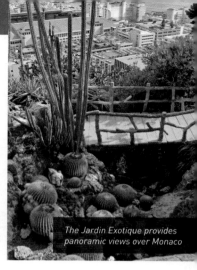

The Jardin Exotique provides panoramic views over Monaco

landscape'; equally beguiling are the villa's architectural attributes including stunning stained glass windows.

EXCURSIONS

CAGNES-SUR-MER

Just 13km (8 miles) west of Nice, **Cagnes-sur-Mer ❹** is a popular excursion for the Niçois for a meal out in the medieval hill village of Haut-de-Cagnes, Renoir's house at Les Collettes, the Hippodrome racecourse and a 3.5km (2-mile) shingle beach. At the top of picturesque Haut-de-Cagnes, with its steep, winding streets of creeper-covered houses, many now containing restaurants and galleries, is the **Château-Musée Grimaldi** (Wed–Mon July–Aug 10am–1pm, 2–6pm, Apr–June and Sept 10am–noon, 2–6pm, Oct–Mar 10am–noon, 2–5pm). This was a watchtower constructed by one of the branches of the Grimaldi family, before being converted into a sumptuous Renaissance residence. A galleried, vaulted loggia leads to a magnificent ceremonial chamber, with a carved fireplace and dramatic 1620 *trompe l'œil* ceiling with the *Fall of Phaethon*, attributed to Genoese painter Giulio Benso Pietra.

The château also contains a small display devoted to the olive tree, the municipal art collection and the surprising Collection Suzy Solidor, donated by the Montparnasse cabaret singer, a former resident of the château, who was painted by many of

⊘ MATISSE'S CHAPEL IN VENCE

During World War II the elderly Matisse retreated to **Vence** (14km/9 miles from Cagnes-sur-Mer) to avoid the bombing, renting Villa Le Rêve, where young Monique Bourgeois (later Sister Jacques Marie) nursed and sat for him. In gratitude he offered to decorate the Chapelle du Rosaire for the Dominican order, and ended up designing everything from the building itself with its blue-and-white glazed pantiles to the priest's cope and the gilded crucifix that stands on the altar. The **Chapelle du Rosaire-Henri Matisse** (avenue Henri Matisse; Tue–Sat 2–6pm, Tue, Thu–Fri also 10am–noon, Nov–Mar until 5pm) is a meeting of Matisse's mastery of line in the pared-back drawings of *St Dominic*, the *Virgin and Child* and *Stations of the Cross* in black on white tiles, and of colour in the stained glass, whose reflections send dapples of blue, yellow and green across the walls. Too ill to attend the opening ceremony, Matisse nonetheless sent along a text: 'This work took four years of assiduous work and is the summary of all my active life. I consider it, despite all its imperfections, as my masterpiece.'

the successful portraitists of the 1920s. This gives the unusual opportunity of seeing the same person depicted by Kisling, Foujita, Van Dongen, Cocteau and Tamara de Lempicka.

The Musée Renoir

Down the hill, east of the modern centre of Cagnes-sur-Mer, the Domaine Les Collettes, now the **Musée Renoir** (Wed–Mon June–Sept 10am–1pm, 2–6pm, Oct–Mar 10am–noon,

Chapelle du Rosaire Henri-Matisse

2–5pm, Apr–May until 6pm), was bought by the elderly Renoir in 1908. Although now surrounded by urban sprawl and apartment blocks that have partly obscured the view, the house and gardens have changed little since Renoir lived here, receiving visitors such as Pierre Bonnard and Matisse, who painted the garden, as well as photographer Willy Maywald, whose photos hang on the stairs.

Paintings around the house include a study for the large *Late Bathers*, its heightened, almost garish, palette no doubt something to do with the Riviera's bright sunshine, which Renoir described as 'maddening'; and a charming small portrait of his youngest son Claude, *Coco Reading*, dressed in a sailor suit that can still be seen hanging in the studio. But Renoir, almost crippled by arthritis, increasingly turned to sculpture, producing small bronzes in collaboration with his assistant Richard Guino (who is credited as co-author) and later with Louis Morel.

MOUGINS

Just 8km (5 miles) inland from Cannes, the chic little hill village of **Mougins** ❺ (www.mougins.fr) is a lively gastronomic night out from Cannes, with some of the best restaurants in the region. On the main square, **place Lamy**, art galleries, craft shops and a clutter of gourmet bistros surround a fountain with a rusty statue of 19th-century explorer Général Lamy, who was born here. Above here pristine stepped *ruelles* wind up to the much-altered Romanesque church with its wrought-iron campanile. Round the corner by the Porte Sarrazine, a fortified 15th-century gateway, the **Musée de la Photographie** (daily Sept–June 10am–12.30pm and 2–6pm, July–Aug 10am–1pm and 2–7pm; free) has a collection of early cameras and a fascinating array of portraits of Picasso, a former resident of Mougins, by Doisneau, Lartigue, Clergue, Villers and others.

Each September, the village hosts a must-visit event for foodies, Les Etoiles de Mougins (www.lesetoilesdemougins.com), when some of the world's best chefs gather to demonstrate their skills and inventions.

THE ESTÉREL

The Estérel massif offers the most astonishing colours on the Riviera and can be travelled in an easy loop from Cannes by coastal N98 one way and A8 or N7 the

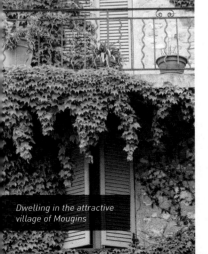

Dwelling in the attractive village of Mougins

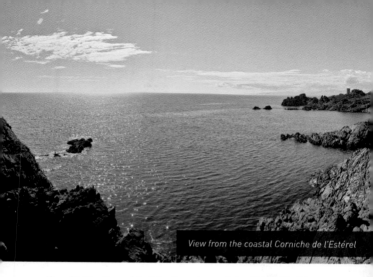

View from the coastal Corniche de l'Estérel

other. Unlike the arid white limestone of the Alpes-Maritimes, here the rock is deep-red porphyry, which contrasts with the Mediterranean blue, with parasol pines, garrigue scrub and the yellow of mimosa in winter. The initial section of coast road nearest to Cannes is highly built up as it passes through La Napoule and Théoule-sur-Mer, but later the scenery becomes more natural. For centuries this was a wild, inaccessible area, terrorised by 18th-century bandit Gaspard de Bresse, a sort of French Robin Hood, from his base at Les Adrets de l'Estérel (now the wrong side of the N7), and the Corniche d'Or road (N98) was constructed by the Touring Club de France only in 1903.

On the shore at **La Napoule ❻**, 8km (5 miles) west of Cannes, the **Château de la Napoule** (www.chateau-lanapoule.com; gardens daily 10am–6pm; guided visits of château early Feb–early Nov daily 11.30am, 2.30pm, 3.30pm, 4.30pm, early Nov–early Feb Mon–Fri 2.30pm, 3.30pm, Sat–Sun 11.30am, 2.30pm, 3.30pm)

Fréjus Old Town

is a too-good-to-be-true medieval castle fancifully restored in the 1920s by eccentric American sculptor Henry Clews, who added extra turrets, a gatehouse and ramparts.

Clews, a scion of a New York banking family, and his wife Marie dressed in period attire and peppered the castle and topiaried gardens with moral mottoes and Henry's imaginative sculptures and gargoyles.

Beyond Théoule-sur-Mer, footpaths lead to the unspoilt **Pointe de l'Aiguille** headland, while at the little harbour of **La Figuierette** several footpaths and forestry tracks head into the interior, climbing to the Pic de l'Ours or to the Col Notre-Dame, where a 12m (40ft) high modern statue of Notre-Dame d'Afrique gazes across the sea to a similar statue in Algeria.

Further west, past Trayas and Cap Roux, the gorgeous creek of **Agay** is a family resort, with a touch of nostalgia for its 1930s heyday. Just off the coast, the Ile d'Or served as model for Hergé's *Tintin et l'Ile Noire*. The nearby Plage du Dramont was one of the main landing beaches for Allied troops from North Africa in the 1944 liberation of Provence.

At the western edge of the massif, **Saint-Raphaël** (www.saint-raphael.com) is a low-key resort focused around its yachting marina and palm-lined seafront, no longer the fashionable destination it was in the late 19th century. More interesting is adjoining

Fréjus ❼ (www.frejus.fr), once the important Roman port of Forum Julii. There's an impressive ruined amphitheatre, now used for bullfighting and concerts, and fragments of the Roman aqueduct on the outskirts, but the gem is the **cathedral complex** (June–Sept daily 10am–12.30pm, 1.45–6.30pm, Oct–May Tue–Sun 10am–1pm, 2–5pm) in the centre of the Old Town. You should take one of the guided tours to see the 5th-century baptistery, the cloister with an unusual wooden ceiling decorated with animals and mythical beasts, and the cathedral's elaborately carved doors.

⊙ VENTURING INLAND

Inland from the coast, the climate changes and the scenery becomes more Alpine. By car from Cannes the Route Napoléon (N85) roughly follows the mountain route taken by Napoleon on his march on Paris after escaping from Elba in 1815. After the perfume town of **Grasse**, the route becomes more grandiose, with views of snow-topped peaks in the distance, crossing St-Vallier-de-Thiey on the stony Plateau de Caussols and forested Escragnolles, before arriving at pretty **Castellane**, known for its strange fossils and perched under a rocky outcrop at the entrance to the spectacular Gorges de Verdon; it then continues to the dignified spa town of **Digne-les-Bains**, and on northwards via fortified Sisteron to Gap. An alternative is to take the **Train des Pignes** (www.trainprovence.com), a scenic narrow-gauge railway between the Gare de Provence in Nice and Digne. Stops include Puget-Théniers, **Entrevaux**, with an imposing citadel high above the River Var, and picturesque **Annot**. Vintage steam trains run between Puget-Théniers and Annot via Entrevaux some Sundays from early May to late Oct (reserve on tel: 04 97 03 80 80).

The Côte d'Azur is a sailor's paradise

WHAT TO DO

Beyond sightseeing and eating out, there are plenty of things to keep the visitor occupied. All three cities offer endless shopping and window-shopping opportunities. In summer, the beach and water sports are the obvious choice for activities, complemented by a host of outdoor music festivals and fireworks displays. The rest of the year the busy agenda ranges from Nice's traditional Carnaval and the Monte Carlo Car Rally to opera and ballet.

SHOPPING

WHAT TO BUY WHERE

Nice, Cannes and Monaco are all major shopping destinations. Cosmopolitan Nice offers the greatest variety, while Cannes and Monaco are firmly targeted at the luxury fashion market, with an adventurous, trendy edge in Cannes and more conservative styles in Monaco.

In Nice, smart designer labels are concentrated along avenue de Suède, avenue de Verdun, rue Paradis and rue Alphonse-Karr, where you'll find Chanel, Emporio Armani, Cartier, Max Mara and Kenzo as well as the 'preppy' men's and women's wear of Nice-based Façonnable. Among more unusual shops, **Kantzé** (10 rue Alphonse-Karr) is hot on the latest trends from designers such as Liu Jo, Not Shy, Kocca and Des Petits Hauts; **Espace Harroch** (7 rue Paradis, www.espace-harroch.com) is a chic multi-level, multi-label outlet for men's and women's clothes, kitchenware and interior design items.

For more mainstream chain stores, go to Rue de France, rue Masséna and avenue Jean-Médecin, home to practical supermarket **Monoprix**, **Fnac** book, music, photo and computer superstore, the **Galeries Lafayette** shopping centre (www. galerieslafayette.com/magasin-nice) and the **Nicetoile** shopping centre (www.nicetoile.com).

In Vieux Nice, food shops and souvenir outlets mix with art and craft galleries, such as **Art Gallery Lepa** (27 rue de la Buffa), New Agey clothes shops, and organic and ethical clothing outlet **Ekyog** (12 rue Alphonse-Karr). **Village Ségurane** is an arcade of 40 antiques dealers on rue Ségurane between place Garibaldi and the Vieux Port.

In Cannes, high-end boutiques are concentrated along La Croisette, rue d'Antibes and the **Gray d'Albion** mall that runs between the two. For diamond necklaces and haute couture dresses suitable for walking up *les marches*, the most prestigious labels (Lacroix, Cartier, Balenciaga, Ferragamo) cluster on La Croisette, with younger styles, such as Paul & Joe, Zadig & Voltaire and Italian labels Missoni and Patrizia Pepe on rue d'Antibes. Rue Meynadier near the food market is lined with outlets for cheaper casual wear and beach gear.

Monaco's 'golden rectangle' is on place du Casino and avenue des Beaux-Arts, which stretches between the Hôtel de Paris and Hôtel Hermitage. **Galerie du Métropole** is an upmarket mall, next to the Hôtel Métropole; more boutiques can be found on avenue Princesse Grace and boulevard des Moulins. Up in Monaco-Ville, the **Chocolaterie de Monaco** (place de la Visitation) is a rare exception to the many souvenir shops. Monégasques go to Fontvieille just for the huge Centre Commercial, home to Carrefour hypermarket, clothing chains and the sports store Decathlon.

FOOD AND WINE

As in any French town, the food market is an essential part of life, and **cours Saleya** market in Vieux Nice, the **Marché Forville** in Cannes and the **Marché de la Condamine** in Monaco are the places for stocking up on fresh produce. Good items to take home include olive oil and related products such as table olives and tapenades. French olive oil production is tiny by

Marché Forville, Cannes

Italian and Spanish standards, but it is usually of high quality. The Nice area has an *appellation d'origine protégée* (AOP) for oil made from its tiny purple cailletier olive. Outlets include **Alziari** (14 rue St-François-de-Paule, www.alziari.com.fr), and **Oliviera** (8 bis rue du Collet, www.oliviera.com), both in Vieux Nice, and stalls in Cannes's Marché Forville.

Also in Vieux Nice, look out for candied fruit and other gourmet items from **Maison Auer** (www.maison-auer.com), truffles at **Terres de Truffes** (www.terresdetruffes.com), both on rue St-François-de-Paule, and home-made pasta from **Maison Barale** (7 rue Sainte-Réparate; www.maison-barale.fr). Other regional produce includes wines from Bellet (see page 106) and the Lérina liqueur made by the monks on Ile Saint-Honorat. The oldest wine shop in Nice is **Cave Bianchi** (7 rue Raoul Bosio, www.cave-bianchi.fr) which also has a branch in Cannes (5 rue du Maréchal-Joffre).

Carnaval de Nice musicians

ARTS AND ENTERTAINMENT

PERFORMING ARTS

While the south of France is often remembered for its summer festivals, both Nice and Monaco have an active year-round arts calendar. In fact, the serious arts season runs from September or October to June; over July and August the performing arts tend to move outdoors, with theatre productions in the Fort Saint-Antoine in Monaco, Nice's renowned jazz festival in Cimiez and electronic music and chamber music events in Cannes.

For information, look out for the culture agenda on www.nice.fr and the free brochures *Sortir à Cannes* (Oct–Apr) and *L'Été à Cannes* (May–Sept), published by the tourist office.

The **Opéra de Monte Carlo** (www.opera.mc) offers a glamorous night out amid the gilt and chandeliers of the opera house. Under director-choreographer Jean-Christophe Maillot the **Ballets de Monte Carlo** (www.balletsdemonte carlo.com), the descendant of Diaghilev's Ballets Russes, has become one of Europe's top troupes. It generally performs in the Grimaldi Forum when not on tour. First-rate contemporary international dance companies take part in the biennial **Cannes Dance Festival** in November (www.festivaldedanse-cannes.com).

The **Opéra de Nice** (www.opera-nice.org) is another fine opera house. It stages a wide range of productions, along with ballet and classical concerts by the respected **Orchestre Philharmonique.** Nice is also home to the **Ensemble Baroque de Nice**, one of France's leading early-music ensembles, and the experimental contemporary music institute CIRM, which organises the **MANCA** festival (www.cirm-manca.org) in November. The **Théâtre National de Nice** (www.tnn.fr), on the promenade des Arts, is the most important of several in Nice. In Cannes, most events take place in the **Palais des Festivals** (www.palaisdesfestivals.com).

ROCK AND JAZZ
Big-name rock bands and French variété singers perform at the vast **Palais Nikaia** (www.nikaia.fr) and **Nice Acropolis**

☉ CARNAVAL DE NICE

For the two weeks leading up to Shrove Tuesday, Nice lets its hair down in the annual Carnaval, a pre-Lenten tradition going back to the Middle Ages – and probably to pagan festivals before. It took its present form in the late 19th century when the municipality organised what had been a raucous event of street dancing and masked balls into a parade of carnival floats. Today, there's a different theme each year as colourfully decorated floats, dancers, musicians and giant carnival figures with papier mâché heads parade noisily each night behind the King of Carnaval, culminating with fireworks on the last night. In the afternoon, thousands of flowers are thrown in the *bataille des fleurs* along the promenade des Anglais. You have to pay for reserved seats along the promenade des Anglais, but you can join the crowds around the Jardins Albert Ier for free (www.nicecarnaval.com).

Convention Centre (www.sean-acropolis.com) in Nice and in the **Grimaldi Forum** in Monaco; the **Théâtre Lino Ventura** (www.nicemusiclive.fr) in Nice has a programme of pop music and contemporary dance; local bands and British indie groups turn up at popular **Wayne's Bar** (15 rue de la Préfecture, www.waynes.fr) in the Old Town. In summer, there are outdoor concerts in the **Théâtre de Verdure** in the Jardin Albert Ier. The **Monte Carlo Sporting Summer Festival** (www.monte carlosbm.com) at the Sporting d'Été features young pop divas along with rock and soul legends.

Nice Jazz Festival (www.nicejazzfestival.fr) in July has a relaxed atmosphere as spectators wander between three stages in the Roman arena and gardens by the Matisse Museum in Cimiez. It encompasses a wide spectrum of music, ranging from celebrated jazz veterans to soul, blues, funk, folk and hip hop.

Out on the town in Cannes

NIGHTLIFE

Cannes offers plenty of sophisticated nightlife. During the film festival, trendy Paris clubs come south and stage parties. In July and August, Hôtel Martinez's chic **Zplage** hosts international DJs, while the **Pantiero** festival focuses on new electronic music trends.

The rest of the year, the hub of trendy lounge bars with DJs is a block back from La Croisette on rue du Docteur Monod and rue des Frères Pratignac, led by **Sun7 Bar** and **For You**. Other regulars include gay bar **Le Vogue** on rue du Suquet, weekend DJ parties at **Hôtel 3.14** and the summer **Le Medusa** at the Palm Beach Casino (http://palmbeachevents. fr). Classy all-night restaurant, sushi bar and

The Casino de Monte Carlo is the ultimate in glamour

discotheque **Le Bâoli** (www.lebaoli.com) on Port Pierre Canto draws a VIP crowd and has a tough door-selection policy.

Nice is curiously short on top club venues. Here nightlife revolves more around an active pub scene, and lounge bars serving finger food. Stalwarts include **Les Trois Diables** (2 cours Saleya, www.les3diables.com), **Au Fût et à Mésure** (2 rue Gilly, www.aufutetamesure.fr), and DJ and cocktail bar the **Ghost House** (3 rue de la Barillerie, www.leghost-pub.com).

Clubbing in Monaco is generally for the affluent. **Jimmy'z** (www. montecarlosbm.com) at the Sporting d'Été is where you'll find the Monaco princesses, racing drivers, rock stars and top models, while **La Rascasse** (quai Antoine Ier) is for all those who enjoy dancing and clubbing all night. There's a more laid-back mood at **Stars 'n' Bars** (see page 114) by the Port Hercule, and for a more traditional piano bar ambience head to the **Sass Café** (11 avenue princesse Grace).

CASINOS

The sumptuous **Casino de Monte Carlo** is the most beautiful and famous of Monte Carlo's assorted casinos, but other options include the **Casino Café de Paris**, where punters crowd the slot machines from 10am until the early hours of the morning (table games from 8pm); fairground-themed **Sun Casino** inside the Fairmont Hotel, which has an emphasis on 'American games' (American roulette, poker, blackjack, craps), while the **Monte Carlo Bay Casino** has high-tech slot machines only. None of Monte Carlo's casinos allow religious or military uniforms (www.montecarlosbm.com).

At Cannes, there are three casinos: **Casino Croisette** (www.groupebarriere.com), in the Palais des Festivals, **Les Princes** (www.groupebarriere.com), in the Palais Stéphanie Hotel, and the **3.14 Casino** (www.314casino.com) at Pointe Croisette, a legendary 1930s venue that reopened in 2002. Nice has two casinos on the promenade des Anglais: at No. 1, glitzy 1970s-style **Casino Ruhl** (www.groupebarriere.com), with slot machines, gaming tables and a Vegas-style revue (weekends except July and Aug); and the revived neo-Art Deco **Palais de la Méditerranée** (No.13, www.casinomediterranee.com).

SPORTS AND ACTIVITIES

BEACHES AND SWIMMING

Private beach concessions provide sun loungers, parasols and changing rooms; some have water-sports facilities and many have restaurants serving excellent food, from classic grilled fish and salads to cosmopolitan modern cuisine. Others morph into cocktail and DJ bars in the evening, while a few provide beauty treatments and massages. In Nice, the long pebble beach has plenty of public areas, with showers and loos, between the private concessions. In Cannes, if you're not paying for a private beach along La Croisette, head to the mainly public **Plage du Mourré Rouge** to the east or **Plage du Midi** to the west. Monaco's **Larvotto Beach** is surprisingly small. You may want to cross the frontier to the unspoilt **Plage Cabbé** at Roquebrune Cap-Martin to the east, where there's also bathing off the rocks from the Sentier du Littoral coast path, or west to Cap d'Ail, where, if you're prepared for a walk down the steps, lovely **Plage Mala** has a spectacular setting in a small bay with mountains descending straight to the sea. Note that topless bathing has gone out of fashion.

SAILING AND WATER SPORTS

Jet skis, parascending and water-skiing are available at several of Cannes' and Nice's private beaches. For dinghy sailing classes and hire, try: **Plongée Aigle Nautique** (50 boulevard Franck-Pilatte, Nice; tel: 06 75 79 13 12, http://plongeeaiglenautique.fr), a water-sports centre on the eastern edge of the Vieux Port.

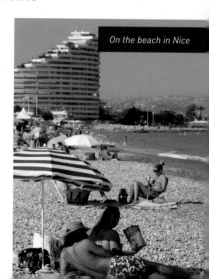

On the beach in Nice

DIVING

The shipwrecks, underwater caves and marine fauna and flora of the

Alpes-Maritimes offer some spectacular diving. Try: **Plongée Aigle Nautique**, Nice; **Nemo Plongée** (Pointe Croisette, Cannes; tel: 04 93 70 49 97; www.nemo-plongee.org), for deep-sea diving courses and expeditions, sea-kayaking classes and equipment hire; or the **Plongée Club de Cannes** (quai St-Pierre, Cannes; tel: 06 11 81 76 17, www.plongee-cannes. com), which offers diving around the Iles de Lérins.

GOLF

The Riviera has some of France's best golf courses. The **Royal Mougins Golf Club** (424 avenue du Roi, Mougins; tel: 04 92 92 49 69, www.royalmougins.fr) has an 18-hole course, plus spa and hotel, just outside Cannes. The **Monte Carlo Golf Club La Turbie** (tel: 04 92 41 50 70, http://golfdemontecarlo.com), is an 18-hole course in a spectacular 900m (2,950ft) setting on Mont Agel.

GYMS AND FITNESS

Many of the upmarket hotels have small gyms and fitness rooms. For a more serious workout and a wide range of exercise classes try **Tropic Gym** (www.tropicgymnice. com) in Nice, and the **Club Moving Nice**, which also has aqua-gym sessions.

SKIING

Nice residents like to boast that they can be on the ski slopes in the morning and on the beach in the afternoon. The nearest ski stations to Nice are **Valberg**

Yachts galore

Vintage yawls, ketches, dragons and other classic racing yachts provide a spectacular vision as they set out across the Baie de Cannes at the end of September in **Les Régates Royales** (www.regatesroyales. com), a regatta founded by the International Yacht Club of Cannes in 1929.

The Monaco Grand Prix

(www.valberg.com), **Auron** (www.auron.com) and **Isola 2000** (www.isola2000.com) in the Mercantour; from Cannes it is easier to reach **Gréolières Les Neiges** (www.greolieres.fr) on the Massif du Cheiron.

TENNIS AND SQUASH

The **Monte Carlo Country Club** (155 avenue Princesse Grace, Roquebrune-Cap Martin; tel: 04 93 41 30 15, www.mccc.mc) is a luxury club with clay tennis courts, squash, pool and gym; day membership is available. The following have courts which can be hired by the hour: **Nice Lawn Tennis Club** (5 avenue Suzanne Lenglen, Nice; tel: 04 92 15 58 00, www.niceltc.com), a century-old private club with lawn and clay courts; **Tennis-Squash Club Vauban** (18 rue Maréchal Vauban, Nice; tel: 04 93 26 09 78, http://tsvauban.free.fr) and **Tennis Club de Cannes** (11 rue Lacour, Cannes; tel: 04 93 43 63 57, www.cannestennis.com).

SPECTATOR SPORTS

The Riviera's biggest sporting event is the **Monaco Grand Prix** in May (see page 68); motor fans also come out for the **Monte Carlo Car Rally** in January, which finishes here after crossing the snow-covered Col de Turini. Nice and Monaco both have premier division **football** teams and Nice was a host city in the UEFA Euro 2016 Football Championship; it will also host the FIFA Women's World Cup in 2019; horse racing takes place at the **Hippodrome de la Côte d'Azur** at Cagnes-sur-Mer just west of Nice. Other events include the **Monte Carlo Tennis Masters** men's singles tournament, international athletics meetings in Nice and Monaco, and international showjumping in Cannes and Monaco. The 1,200km (745-mile) **Paris–Nice cycling race** in

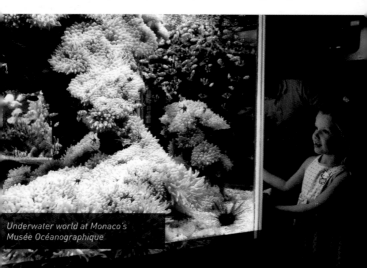

*Underwater world at Monaco's
Musée Océanographique*

mid-March, which finishes on the promenade des Anglais, is one of the big events of the international cycling calendar.

CHILDREN

Nice's beach is a draw for children, although it is pebbly and shelves steeply; some private beaches have children's pools and sandpits. Treats include ice creams from **Fenocchio** (see page 30) on place Rossetti and rue de la Poissonnerie. The **Parc Floral Phoenix** (see page 45) has plenty to keep kids amused, with an otter pool, aquariums with fish and spiders and a musical fountain. Local families also like the **Castel des Deux Rois**, east of the Vieux Port, which has good playgrounds, mini golf and water jets.

The main attractions at Cannes are the beach and the summer fireworks displays. **Ile Sainte-Marguerite** (see page 61) makes an ideal family day out, with beaches, picnic spots and an enjoyable boat trip at either end. There are also trips to be taken around the bay in glass-bottomed boats.

The aquarium (containing around 100 tanks) in Monaco's **Musée Océanographique** (see page 74) is popular with families but gets crowded in July and August. The **Jardin Animalier** (see page 76) has over 250 exotic animals from 50 species, who have all been given to the zoo and are kept in good conditions.

The area's biggest attraction is **Marineland** (daily 10am–7pm, July–Aug until 10pm; www.marineland.fr) between Antibes and Biot. Highlights are the whale and dolphin shows, but the complex also includes Aquasplash water park, Adventure Golf and Kid's Island, with baby farm animals and pony rides.

CALENDAR OF EVENTS

January Monaco: Monte Carlo Car Rally cars hurtle from the Alps to the principality; Monaco Circus Festival; *Fête de Sainte-Dévote*.

February Nice: *Carnaval de Nice* (see page 89).

March Nice: Paris–Nice cycle race; *Festin des Cougourdins* in Cimiez, a religious procession accompanied by engraved and painted gourds.

April Monaco: *Printemps des Arts* classical music and theatre festival; Monte Carlo Tennis Masters men's singles championship.

May Cannes: International Film Festival. Monaco: Monaco Grand Prix.

June France-wide (21st): *Fête de la Musique* free concerts, mostly outdoors. Nice: *Festival du Livre* literary festival; *Festival de la Musique Sacrée*. Monaco: international showjumping.

July France-wide (14th): Bastille Day, with dancing and fireworks. Nice: Nice Jazz Festival – first-rate performers in the Roman amphitheatre at Cimiez; festival lasts a week, usually in the second half of the month.

July–August Nice: *La Castellada* promenade spectacle on the castle hill. Cannes: Pantiero electronic music festival; *Les Nuits Musicales du Suquet* chamber music in front of the church; *Festival d'art pyrotechnique* spectacular fireworks. Monaco: Monte Carlo Sporting Summer Festival – big-name pop, rock and soul stars perform at the Sporting d'Été; *Cinéma d'Été* outdoor cinema on a giant screen.

August Monaco: fireworks festival.

September France-wide (3rd weekend): *Journées du Patrimoine* heritage days. Cannes: International Yachting Festival luxury yacht salon, followed by *Les Régates Royales* classic yacht racing.

October Monaco: *Prix International d'Art Contemporain* winner's exhibition.

November Nice and Monaco: MANCA contemporary music festival. Monaco (18th, 19th): *Fête Nationale*. Nice and Cannes: *Marathon des Alpes-Maritimes*, a scenic run between the promenade des Anglais in Nice and the Palais des Festivals in Cannes. Cannes: dance festival (odd years).

December Nice: *Lou Presèpi-Calena* is a live Christmas nativity play on place Rossetti.

EATING OUT

The south of France's exceptional local produce is at the heart of the cuisine here. Much of the best cooking is seasonal: asparagus in spring, tomatoes and courgettes in summer, tarts and gratins made with fresh figs in late summer, game, wild mushrooms and truffles in autumn.

REGIONAL SPECIALITIES

Olive oil rather than butter is used for cooking and is a crucial ingredient in *anchoïade* (also known as *bagna cauda*), a warm anchovy and olive oil sauce, into which chopped raw vegetables are dipped, and *aïoli* (garlic mayonnaise), which usually appears as an appetiser dip.

Nice's distinctive cuisine is a fusion of Provençal and Italianate influences resulting from the town's Savoyard past and a long to-and-fro history between the two, as well as its market-gardening tradition. Some specialities, such as *salade niçoise* (salad with tuna, olives, peppers, green beans, eggs and anchovies) and *ratatouille* (a hearty, luscious mixture of tomatoes, onions, garlic, courgettes, peppers and

Salade niçoise

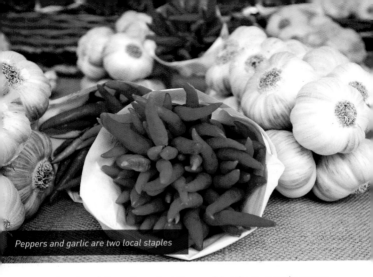

Peppers and garlic are two local staples

aubergines), have travelled the world; others remain essentially local.

Nice claims to have invented ravioli, but here, unlike those found in Italy, they are typically filled with leftover *daube de bœuf* (beef stewed in red wine and herbs, cooked in a *daubière*) and swiss chard. Other Italianate specialities include gnocchi, made from potatoes or durum wheat, and *soupe au pistou*, a rich, minestrone-like vegetable and bean soup into which a sauce of basil, garlic and olive oil (pesto) is stirred at the end.

Nice's *cailletier* olive turns up in many dishes; indeed, *à la niçoise* on a menu will often indicate a sauce made with tomatoes, onions and black olives, and may be found accompanying pasta, fish, chicken or rabbit.

Perhaps the most characteristic of all Niçois dishes, however, is *petits farcis niçois*, an assortment of stuffed tomatoes, aubergines, courgettes, onions and bell peppers, each with its own slightly different filling, based around ham, rice, herbs, minced meat and breadcrumbs.

VEGETABLE HEAVEN

One area where Niçois and Provençal cuisine differ from the rest of France is the emphasis on vegetables, thanks both to the variety and quality of local produce and to peasant tradition where meat was mainly reserved for special occasions. Preparations can be as gloriously simple as marinated and roasted red peppers, or the fresh herbs and varied young salad leaves of delicate *mesclun*. Tomatoes are an ingredient in numerous sauces, but also appear as simple salads and chilled summer soups or as *tomates provençales*, a popular accompaniment to meat and fish dishes, sprinkled with

☺ PORTABLE TREATS

Snack food is an art form in Nice, where a whole range of specialities just seem designed for eating in the street. *Socca*, one of the legendary dishes sold at stalls in Vieux Nice (best-known are Chez René Socca at 1 rue Pairolière and Chez Thérésa in cours Saleya market), is a thin chickpea crêpe cooked on a large circular iron plaque, then cut up into portions, seasoned with black pepper, and best served very hot; *pissaladière* is a delicious open onion tart, garnished with anchovy fillets and black olives. Then there are *panisses*, deep-fried chickpea flour fritters, and *ganses*, mini doughnuts flavoured with orange blossom water and dusted with icing sugar, traditionally eaten during the Carnaval period. Even *salade niçoise* has its portable version, the *pan bagnat*: a crusty roll rubbed with garlic and olive oil and crammed with lettuce, tomato, onion, tuna and anchovies.

Fresh seafood is a regional speciality

minced garlic and breadcrumbs and baked very slowly until almost caramelised. Look out also for *caponata*, aubergine stewed with tomatoes and capers.

You'll also find all manner of vegetable *tians*, baked gratins of courgette, squash or aubergine with egg and rice, named after the rectangular earthenware dish in which they are cooked. Tiny purple artichokes, almost without a choke, are braised *à la barigoule* with mushrooms and bacon, but are also sliced very finely and eaten raw. Another treat is delicate orangey-yellow courgette flowers, dipped in egg and flour and deep-fried as fritters or stuffed with *brousse* (fresh cheese). *Blettes* (swiss chard) are served as a vegetable or combined with apples, raisins and pine kernels in Nice's *tourte de blettes*, a surprisingly sweet tart; while stuffed cabbage, the leaves bound around a sausage-meat filling, is a rustic speciality of the Cannes and Grasse area.

FISH AND MEAT

Not surprisingly, given the Côte d'Azur's glorious coastline and the trend for healthy eating, fish plays a large role, especially at beach restaurants and around the Vieux Port in Nice. However, overfishing of the Mediterranean and the decline of the Riviera's fishing fleet mean that apart from the grandest restaurants, which still buy directly from the remaining local fishermen, much of the fish now comes from France's Breton and Atlantic ports.

Sardines are a speciality in Nice, stuffed with Swiss chard, marinated or grilled, as is *estocaficada* (*stockfisch* in Cannes, *stocafi* in Monaco), salt cod stewed in wine with tomatoes and olives. You'll find the fish stew *bouillabaisse* (originally from Marseille) all along the coast, served in two courses, first the saffron-coloured soup accompanied by a garlicky *rouille* and then the fish and potatoes. Other typical preparations include sea bream baked with fennel and red mullet with basil, as well as grander dishes like sea bass baked in a crust of sea salt. For a brief period in spring look out for the local delicacy *poutine*, the tiny fry of sardines and anchovies fished with nets on the beach (now authorised only between 15 February and 31 March), which is prepared in soup, omelettes or fritters.

Meat is not forgotten, however – this is France. Almost every brasserie will have a *steak frites* on its menu, or a succulent Provençal *daube de bœuf*, stewed in red wine and herbs with a touch of orange zest. Rabbit is also commonly

Meal times

Lunch is served from noon–2.30pm and dinner from 7–10pm. The standard French meal consists of an *entrée* (starter), *plat* (main course) and dessert. Bread and a jug of tap water (*carafe d'eau*) with the meal will be served free on request. Most restaurants offer good-value set menus of two or three courses at lunchtime.

Find French cheeses in the southern markets

found, roasted with herbs or cooked *à la niçoise* with white wine, olives and tomatoes. The best lamb comes from the Alpine hinterland, notably Sisteron, while a more challenging Provençal classic is *pieds et paquets*, stuffed sheep's tripe and feet stewed for hours in a tomato sauce.

CHEESE AND DESSERTS

The Côte d'Azur is not a major cheese-making area, but you will find some mountain-style cow's-milk cheeses from the Mercantour as well as goat's cheese (*chèvre*), ranging from young, moist, fresh cheeses to harder, drier *crottins*. Among specialities are *poivre d'âne*, goat's cheese rolled in summer savory, tiny cheeses marinated in olive oil and herbs, and *brousse*, a ricotta-like fresh cheese used in dips and desserts.

Desserts are mostly based around fruit, including figs baked in tarts, gratins and crumbles, and lemon meringue tart (*tarte au citron meringuée*) made with little lemons from nearby Menton. Fashionable desserts include summer-fruit soups and creations inspired by nostalgia for children's caramel bars and strawberry sweets.

WHERE TO EAT

Restaurants in France range from informal bistros with a convivial atmosphere, tightly packed tables and regional specialities, via modern gourmet bistros and fashionable designer venues, to grand haute-cuisine establishments, with superb cooking, starched linen and formal service.

Brasseries typically keep long hours – some serve all day – and have a lively atmosphere and a menu of classics, such as grilled fish and meat or gleaming platters of oysters and shellfish. There are also numerous Italian restaurants, ranging from popular pizzerias to authentic trattorias. At lunch, the French will often eat casually in a café, perhaps the *plat du jour* (hot dish of the day) or a salad, and even in smarter restaurants may opt for just a starter and main course or main course and dessert rather than all three.

Many restaurants in Vieux Nice and Le Suquet in Cannes remain firmly attached to tradition, with checked tablecloths and menus of regional specialities that don't seem to have changed for decades, but, happily, southern cuisine continues to evolve. In Nice's New Town, a growing number of chefs, often with an haute-cuisine background, are making adventurous use of regional produce and bringing in cosmopolitan influences. For instance, Keisuke Matsushima (see page 109), is Japanese and trained with Régis Marcon and the Pourcel twins, while Luc Salsedo worked at Alain Ducasse's Le Louis XV (see page 113) and the Chèvre d'Or in Eze but has chosen to go for a market menu that changes every 10 days. At such places, you might find modern experimental preparations alongside a return to roots, with slow cooking in cast-iron casseroles.

Grand haute-cuisine establishments, such as Le Chantecler in Nice and Le Louis XV in Monte Carlo (see page 113), remain a pinnacle for special-occasion dining with luxurious ingredients and splendid settings, but Alain Llorca, formerly of Hôtel Negresco and the Moulin de Mougins, runs the Café Llorca (see page 112) in Monaco which has a bar and tea-room as well as a restaurant and even does take-aways.

A notable trend in Nice is for wine bars and wine bistros, where one feature is well-chosen wines available by the glass. Old-style wine bars concentrated largely on simple plates of charcuterie and cheeses, but the new breed often produce adventurous modern dishes but served in a less formal atmosphere than in conventional restaurants.

WHAT TO DRINK

Something you'll probably only ever see on a wine list in Nice are the rare Bellet wines, produced on the outskirts of the city. Most wine lists will also have a good choice from the rest of Provence, including Côtes de Provence, in all three colours; vast quantities of light, summery rosé; more substantial Bandol wines and the southern Rhône appellations – Côtes du Lubéron, Châteauneuf-du-Pape and Côteaux d'Aix-en-Provence. As well as 75cl bottles, wine bars will often have a good choice by the glass, while bistros may offer wines in 25cl or 50cl carafes.

TO HELP YOU ORDER...

Do you have a table? **Avez-vous une table?**
I'd like some... **Je voudrais du/de la/des...**
The bill, please **L'addition, s'il vous plaît**

bread **pain**	pepper **poivre**
butter **beurre**	salt **sel**
cheese **fromage**	sugar **sucre**
coffee **café**	tea **thé**
fish **poisson**	water **de l'eau**
fruit **fruit**	mineral water **eau minérale**
ice cream **glace**	still **plate**
meat **viande**	fizzy **gazeuse**
milk **lait**	wine **vin**

MENU READER

agneau lamb
ail garlic
ananas pineapple
anchois anchovy
asperges asparagus
bar sea bass
beignet fritter
blette swiss chard
bœuf beef
cabillaud cod
caille quail
canard duck
câpre caper
cerise cherry
champignon mushroom
chou cabbage
crevette prawn/shrimp
daube stew
daurade sea bream
dinde turkey
épinards spinach
espadon swordfish
farci stuffed
fève broad bean
foie liver
fraises strawberries
framboises raspberries
friture whitebait
fruits de mer shellfish
gibier game
homard lobster

huîtres oysters
jambon ham
lapin rabbit
légumes vegetables
lotte monkfish
loup sea bass
morue salt cod
œufs eggs
pâte pastry
pâtes pasta
pêche peach
poire pear
poireau leek
pomme apple
pomme de terre potato
porc pork
poulet chicken
poulpe octopus
prune plum
pruneau prune
raisin grape
rascasse scorpion fish
riz rice
rognons kidneys
saucisse sausage
saumon salmon
thon tuna
truite trout
veau veal
velouté creamy soup
volaille poultry

PLACES TO EAT

We have used the following symbols to give an idea of the price for a three-course dinner, without wine, or the most commonly taken set-price menu:

€€€€ over 60 euros
€€€ 40–60 euros
€€ 25–40 euros
€ below 25 euros

NICE

L'Ane Rouge €€€ *7 quai des Deux-Emmanuels, 06300 Nice, tel: 04 93 89 49 63, www.anerougenice.com.* The most reputed of the portside venues, where Michel Devillers serves inventive starters and more classic mains; an emphasis on fish, and surprisingly gutsy flavours. Good, rather formal service. Closed Wed and lunch Thu.

Auberge de Théo €€ *52 avenue Cap de Croix, 06100 Nice, tel: 04 93 81 26 19, www.auberge-de-theo.com.* This cheerful Italian trattoria, with an amusing rustic decor of hayracks, farm implements and Neapolitan crib figures, is one of the rare restaurants in Cimiez. Authentic dishes include mixed antipasti, pasta with swordfish, beef tagliata and little babas doused in limoncello. French and Italian wines. Closed Sun and Mon.

Le Boudoir €€€ *10 rue Chauvain (off Espace Masséna), 0600 Nice, tel: 04 93 87 55 54, www.leboudoirnice.fr.* Very stylish restaurant with a slightly Baroque decor specialising in truffles and foie gras served in many original ways. Extensive wine list. Open for lunch and dinner. Closed Wed.

Citrus €€€ *7 rue Sainte Reparate, 06300 Nice, tel: 04 93 16 27 93, www. citrusnice.fr.* Conveniently located in the Old Town, this small cosy restaurant specialises in Mediterranean cuisine. Chef Philippe Limoges serves up mouth-watering, mostly French dishes, with a twist, including excellent chateaubriand, steaks and duck. Closed Tue and daily lunch.

L'Escalinada €€ *22 rue Pairolière, 06300 Nice, tel: 04 93 62 11 71*. The two whitewashed dining rooms and much-prized terrace are always packed at this Vieux Nice shrine to traditional Niçois specialities, where timeless recipes include sardines *à l'escabèche*, stuffed courgette flowers, gnocchi, plus a very good lemon meringue tart. No credit cards.

Flaveur €€–€€€ *25 rue Gubernatis (off boulevard Dubouchage), 06000 Nice, tel: 04 93 62 53 95,* www.restaurant-flaveur.com. The Tourteaux brothers, formerly of Hôtel Negresco and Keisuke Matsushima, have brought the Provençal and Japanese influences to their own outlandishly decorated restaurant. Lightly poached salmon with avocado and Granny Smith salsa gives a taste of what's to come. Closed Sat lunch, Sun and Mon.

Le Fonétic €€€ *107 Boulevard de Cessole, 06100 Nice, tel: 04 92 07 04 71,* www.lefonetic.com. Try a sea bass fillet with rice and ratatouille or frogs legs at this not very touristy restaurant serving traditional French dishes with a modern twist. Good wines; attentive service. Closed Sun.

Grand Café de Turin €€ *5 place Garibaldi, 06300 Nice, tel: 04 93 62 29 52,* www.cafedeturin.fr. This seafood brasserie has been shucking oysters for over a century, drawing a faithful Niçois clientele despite sometimes grouchy service. The speciality is lavish platters of *fruits de mer*, where oysters, crabs and prawns are accompanied by some rarer treats, such as the *violet* (sea potato) and *oursins* (sea urchins) in winter.

Keisuke Matsushima €€–€€€€ *22 ter rue de France, 06000 Nice, tel: 04 93 82 26 06,* www.keisukematsushima.com. Japan meets Provence with brilliant young chef Keisuke Matsushima, who trained with some of France's top chefs. Subtly lit slate tables and geometrical lines provide a suitable setting for his beautifully presented creations – think green, purple and wild asparagus with lemon froth or scallops with truffles, peas and wasabi. There's a good-value lunch menu if you want to sample his style. Closed Mon and Sat lunch and Sun.

Lou Pistou €€ *4 rue Raoul Bosio (by the law courts), 06000 Nice, tel: 04 93 62 21 82,* www.loupistou.com. This old-fashioned bistro with checked table cloths and colourful posters on the wall paying homage to Beaujolais Nouveau is a favourite with locals who pack the small dining room to savour well-prepared *Niçois* cuisine. Closed Sat–Sun.

La Maison de Marie €€ *5 rue Masséna, 06000 Nice, tel: 04 93 82 15 93,* www.lamaisondemarie.com. Set back from the street with tables in a quiet courtyard or in an elegant dining room. A stylish take on French and Mediterranean favourites ranges from foie gras, stuffed sardines and herb-encrusted lamb to pasta with scampi. Look for some good Corsican bottles among the Provençal ones on the wine list.

Restaurant du Gesù € *place du Gesù, 06000 Nice, tel: 04 93 62 26 46.* Cheap and cheerful local and Italian specialities in a picturesque setting in the shadow of the Eglise du Gesù in Vieux Nice. On warm days, munch a pizza – reputedly the best in Nice – on the terrace and watch the world go by. Closed Sun.

La Roustide €€€ *34 rue Beaumont, 06000 Nice, tel: 04 93 89 69 60,* www. laroustide.fr. Small restaurant with a modern Provençal decor. The chef specialises in artful truffle dishes. The five-course tasting menu is really worth a try. Closed Mon and Sun.

Le Safari €€ *1 cours Saleya, 06000 Nice, tel: 04 93 80 18 44,* www.restaurant safari.fr. This market-side brasserie is a Niçois institution, with a great people-watching terrace. Friendly high-speed waiters serve pretty good renditions of local specialities (*salade niçoise*, rabbit, artichoke salad), plus grilled meats and wood-oven-cooked pizzas.

Yolo Wine Bar €€ *10 rue du Maréchal-Joffre, 06000 Nice, tel: 04 93 88 53 07.* Large, stylish open-plan bar with a great atmosphere. An extensive wine list plus a selection of sushi, cheese and meat platters. Hip lounge music.

CANNES

Astoux et Brun €€ *27 avenue Félix Faure, 06400 Cannes, tel: 04 93 39 21 87,* www.astouxbrun.com. This famous seafood venue behind the port is extremely popular for both its oysters and grandiose shellfish platters and for the people-watching opportunities outside.

Aux Bons Enfants € *80 rue Meynadier, 06400 Cannes, tel: 06 18 81 37 47*, www.aux-bons-enfants-cannes.com. In a busy backstreet between the port and the market, this simple bistro has been in the same family since 1934, serving comforting home-cooked regional food such as grilled sardines and herby Sisteron lamb with courgettes or Swiss chard. Closed Sun–Mon. No credit cards.

L'Assiette Provençale €€ *9 Quai Saint-Pierre, 06400 Cannes, tel: 04 93 38 52 14*, www.assiette-provencale.fr. Located in Cannes' old port, this moderately-priced restaurant serves up excellent Provençal fare. Three-course set menus available for €26 and €31 are really worth a try.

Le Bistrot des Anges €€ *rue de l'Ouest, 06110 Le Cannet, tel: 04 92 18 18 28*, www.bruno-oger.com. A short walk from the Musée Bonnard, this stylish bistro in an 18th-century farmhouse is the more affordable of celebrated chef Bruno Oger's two restaurants. The terrace of the Ange Bar is the perfect place for pre- or post-meal drinks.

Le Relais des Semailles €€ *9–11 rue St-Antoine, Le Suquet, 06400 Cannes, tel: 04 93 39 22 32*, www.lerelaisdessemailles.com. White linen and exposed stone walls provide a pretty setting at this upmarket bistro on Le Suquet's main street. The emphasis is on seasonal ingredients from Forville market. Modern Provençal dishes might include grilled squid in frothy seafood sauce and roast veal with artichokes. Good if pricey wine list. Closed Mon lunch.

Table 22 €€–€€€ *22 rue St-Antoine, Le Suquet, 06400 Cannes, tel: 04 93 39 13 10*, www.restaurantmantel.com. An acclaimed gourmet spot in the Old Town for chef Noël Mantel's elegant southern cooking, such as stuffed vegetables, courgette-flower fritters and fish baked in sea salt. Closed Tue–Wed dinner and Mon.

La Table du Chef €–€€ *5 rue Jean Daumas, 06400 Cannes, tel: 04 93 68 27 40*. Small restaurant off the rue d'Antibes where fresh produce from Forville market is transformed into delicious Mediterranean cuisine – like sea bass with crystallised lemons. Closed Sun, Mon and Tue morning.

La Tonnelle €€–€€€ *Ile Saint-Honorat, 06414 Cannes, tel: 04 92 99 54 08*, http://tonnelle-abbayedelerins.fr. Take a boat trip out to the smaller of the two Lérins Islands for a waterside lunch with wonderful views over the coast. Don't forget to try the wine made by the monks of the Abbaye de Lérins. A cheaper snack bar is open from May to September.

La Toque d'Or €€ *11 rue Louis Blanc, 06400 Cannes, tel: 04 93 39 68 08*. A small friendly restaurant run by two young chefs. A great place to try beautifully served French food. The famous "chocolate bomb" dessert is not to be missed. Open for lunch and dinner. Closed Mon.

MONACO

Café Llorca €€€ *First floor, Grimaldi Forum, 10 avenue Princesse Grace, 98000 Monaco, tel: +377 99 99 29 29*, www.cafellorca.mc. Stylish restaurant, bar and tea room complex from one of the Riviera's best-known chefs, Alain Llorca. The traditional menu includes salt-baked cod followed by chocolate and raspberry tart. Open for lunch only.

Café de Paris €€€ *place du Casino, 98000 Monaco, tel: +377 98 06 76 23*, www.montecarlosbm.com. A faithful recreation of the original Belle Epoque bar and brasserie, next to the Casino. Great people-watching on the pavement terrace, plus a restaurant with 1900s decor and slot machines. The crêpe Suzette was invented here, they say. Serves food all day.

Castelroc €€ *place du Palais, Monaco Ville, 98000 Monaco, tel: +377 93 30 36 68*, www.castelrocmonaco.com. This institution in Monaco-Ville, with cheerfully frescoed dining room and terrace facing the palace, is the place to try Monaco's Italianate specialities, such as *stocafi* (stockfish). Closed Mon.

Joël Robuchon Monte Carlo €€€€ *Hôtel Métropole, 4 avenue de la Madone, Monte Carlo, tel: +377 93 15 15 15*, www.joel-robuchon.com. Joël Robuchon has exported his luxury tapas formula from Paris to Monaco in the hands of emissary Christophe Cusset. Dine on a variety of beautifully prepared, inventive mini dishes, such as artichokes with squid and chorizo. Closed Wed.

Le Louis XV €€€€ *Hôtel de Paris, place du Casino, Monte Carlo, 98000 Monaco, tel: +377 98 06 88 64*, www.ducasse-paris.com. One of the most glamorous restaurants in Europe. Sumptuous decor and immaculate service. The acclaimed cooking by Ducasse, now in the hands of his protégé Dominique Lory, takes Mediterranean cooking to the heights of haute cuisine. Advance booking necessary. Closed Tue, Wed and Thu lunch (open Wed in July–Aug).

La Montgolfière Henri Geraci €€€ *16 rue Basse, 98000 Monaco, tel: +377 97 98 61 59*, www.lamontgolfiere.mc. Simple yet exquisite dishes by chef Henri Geraci are always prepared from fresh local ingredients, so the restaurant's menu changes seasonally. Fusion of French and Asian cuisine. Closed Wed and Sun.

La Note Bleue €€€ *Plage Larvotto, avenue Princesse Grace, 98000 Monaco, tel: +377 93 50 05 02*, www.lanotebleue.mc. This excellent beach restaurant with stylish decor is a relaxed place for lunch under a parasol. Well-prepared, modern Mediterranean-style dishes include plenty of grilled fish. On summer weekends there are free jazz concerts in the evening from quality ensembles.

La Petit Bar €€ *35 rue Basse, 98000 Monaco, tel: +377 97 70 04 97*. This lovely little restaurant in a pedestrianised street in old Monaco is an ideal place to taste authentic Mediterranean fare. Popular with locals and tourists alike. Closed Sat. In winter dinner by reservation only.

Pulcinella €–€€ *17 rue du Portier, 98000 Monaco, tel: +377 93 30 73 61*, www.pulcinella.mc. Tucked away down a side street off the boulevard du Larvotto, this Monaco institution has been serving up Italian food to racing drivers, film stars and the jet set for more than 30 years.

Quai des Artistes €€€ *4 quai Antoine I, La Condamine, 98000 Monaco, tel: +377 97 97 97 77,* www.quaidesartistes.com. Decorated in the style of Parisian brasseries, with a terrace overlooking Port Hercule, this restaurant specialises in traditional Mediterranean cuisine with a special focus on seafood.

Stars 'n' Bars €€ *6 quai Antoine I, La Condamine, 98000 Monaco, tel: +377 97 97 95 95,* www.starsnbars.com. Burgers and Tex-Mex are the name of the game at this popular American restaurant and sports bar. There are inside and outdoor tables overlooking Port Hercule. A friendly welcome for all from small children to racing drivers and pop stars. Service all day.

Le Tip Top € *11 avenue des Spélugues, Monte Carlo, 98000 Monaco, tel: +377 93 50 69 13.* The sort of jovial old-fashioned restaurant and bar that surprisingly does still exist in Monte Carlo. It feeds steak and matchstick chips, plates of spaghetti and pizzas to local workers at lunch and to absolutely everyone (including, to judge from the photos behind the bar, Formula 1 drivers and Prince Albert II) in the dead of night.

EXCURSIONS
Cagnes-sur-Mer

Josy-Jo €€€ *2 rue du Planastel, 06800 Haut-de-Cagnes, tel: 04 93 20 68 76,* www.restaurant-josyjo.com. In an old village house where Modigliani and Soutine once stayed, self-taught chef Josy Bandecchi has made home cooking an art. The speciality is char-grilled meat, followed by Menton lemon mousse or dark chocolate cake. Closed Sun and Mon.

Vence

Les Bacchanales €€€–€€€€ *247 avenue de Provence, 06140 Vence, tel: 04 93 24 19 19,* www.lesbacchanales.com. Contemporary decor and modern Mediterranean cooking in a 19th-century building near Matisse's chapel. There's a year-round events calendar including live jazz on Friday evenings. Closed Tue, Wed and Thu lunch.

Mougins

La Place de Mougins €€€–€€€€ *place du Commandant Lamy, 06250 Mougins Village, tel: 04 93 90 15 78*, www.laplacedemougins.com. Chic bistro in an old village house where each month the chef designs a menu around a specific local product such as a peach or tomato. Alternatively, try something from the *carte* like roast lobster with fig butter followed by Grand Marnier soufflé. Closed Tue and Wed.

Le Rendez-Vous de Mougins € *place du Commandant Lamy, 06250 Mougins Village, tel: 04 93 75 87 47*, www.rendezvousdemougins.com. Amid the cluster of restaurants on the village square, the Rendez-Vous serves simple Provençal food in a convivial atmosphere, 365 days a year.

A–Z TRAVEL TIPS

A SUMMARY OF PRACTICAL INFORMATION

A

ACCOMMODATION (See also Youth Hostels, and the list of Recommended Hotels on page 135)

Hotels. Nice and Cannes have an impressive range of accommodation to suit all budgets. Monaco has a more limited number of mainly large luxury hotels. All three cities, year-round resorts, become very booked up in July and August and during major events. In late May, during Cannes Film Festival and the Monaco Grand Prix, hotels for miles around hike up their prices and are often booked months ahead.

France has an official rating system from one to five stars, based and establishments must invest in the necessary upgrades to ensure they retain their current stars or qualify for a higher rating. Even most two-star hotels now have en suite bathrooms and air conditioning. Luxury hotels will have 24-hour room service and offer all sorts of services, from DVD players and business centres to yacht and helicopter hire.

If booking ahead, the hotel may ask for a deposit, or *arrhes*, but is more likely to request your credit card number. Reservations will usually be honoured until 6pm, but may be given to another client if you have not arrived, or telephoned to explain, before that time.

If looking for last-minute accommodation, the tourist offices in Nice, Cannes and Monaco have a direct booking service.

Most hotels in Nice and Cannes are independently owned, though some are affiliated to groups, such as Best Western (www.bestwestern.com), Châteaux & Hôtels Collection (www.chateauxhotels.com) and Leading Hotels of the World (www.lhw.com). There are also hotels belonging to the Accor group (Sofitel, Mercure, Novotel, Ibis, Adagio; www.accorhotels.com) and Louvre Hotels (Kyriad, Campanile, Golden Tulip, Première Classe chains; www.louvrehotels.com). The majority of Monaco hotels belong to the Société des Bains de Mer de Monaco (www.montecarlosbm.com) or to international groups.

Chambres d'hôtes are bed and breakfast rooms in a private home – enquire at the tourist office.

Appart'hôtels/Résidences de tourisme/Résidences hôtelières. Complexes of holiday studios and apartments, with kitchens.

Villas and seaside flats. Numerous agencies rent villas and holiday flats, ranging from luxury villas with maid service to simple studios.

> Do you have a single/double room for tonight? **Avez-vous une chambre simple/double pour ce soir?**
> with double/twin beds **avec un grand lit/avec deux lits**
> with bath/shower/toilet **avec bain/douche/toilettes**
> What is the rate per night? **Quel est le prix pour une nuit?**

AIRPORT

Aéroport Nice-Côte d'Azur (NCE), on the western edge of Nice, is France's second-busiest airport (tel: 08 20 42 33 33/04 89 88 98 28, www.nice.aeroport.fr). There are connections to all major European cities, North Africa and some American cities. There are numerous flights from the UK with both national and low-cost airlines:

Air France (UK tel: 0207 660 0337, France tel: 3654, www.airfrance. com) flights from Paris.

Aer Lingus (Ireland tel: 1890 800 600, France tel: 0821 23 02 67, www. aerlingus.com) flights from Dublin (seasonal).

British Airways (UK tel: 0844 493 0787, France tel: 08 25 82 54 00, www. britishairways.com) flights from London Heathrow, Gatwick and City.

easyJet (UK tel: 0330 365 5000, France tel: 0806 141 141, www.easyjet. com) flights from Gatwick, Liverpool, Luton and Stansted.

Jet2 (tel: 0333 300 0404, France tel: 0821 230 203, www.jet2.com) flights from Stansted, Leeds Bradford and Manchester (seasonal).

Ryanair (Ireland tel: 1520 444004, France tel: 08 92 562 150, www.ryanair. com) flights from Stansted and Dublin.

Transport from the airport

RCA buses depart from Nice airport for all main destinations along the coast. Buy tickets before boarding at the car park/bus cash desk inside the terminals. Free shuttle between terminals and car parks.

Line 98 from Terminals 1 and 2 direct to Nice centre (Promenade des Arts), daily 5.40am–11.45pm.

Line 99 from Terminals 1 and 2 direct to Nice railway station (Gare SNCF), daily 7.53am–8.53pm.

Line 110 Aéroport–Monte Carlo–Menton Express along the motorway from Terminal 1, daily 8.30am–9pm.

Line 210 to Cannes by RN7 from Terminal 1, daily 8am–8pm.

Taxi with Central Taxi Riviera from Terminals 1 and 2, tel: 04 93 13 78 78; typical fares central Nice €23–31, Cannes €70–75, Monaco €75–80.

Motorbike taxi with Easy Moov (tel: 04 93 00 12 66, www.easy-moov. fr), set fares: Nice airport to Nice €30, to Cannes €70, to Monaco €80.

Heli Air Monaco (tel: +377-92 05 00 50, www.heliairmonaco.com) scheduled helicopter services between Nice airport and Monaco take 7 minutes, and are not necessarily more expensive than a taxi. Nice–Monaco from €133; Monaco–Nice from €133; return trip from €236.

B

BICYCLE HIRE

Elite Rent a Bike 32 avenue Maréchal Juin, Cannes, tel: 04 93 94 30 34 and 6 rue Massenet, Nice, tel: 04 93 04 15 36, www.elite-rentabike.com. Bicycles, scooters and motorbikes.

Holiday Bikes 34 avenue Auber and 6 rue Massenet, Nice, tel: 04 93 16 01 62 and 04 93 04 15 36 respectively; 19 avenue Maréchal Juin, Cannes, tel: 04 97 06 30 63, www.loca-bike.fr. Bicycles, electricity-assisted bikes, scooters and motorbikes.

Rent Bike Palais de la Scala, Galerie Commerciale, 1 avenue Henri Dunant, Monaco, tel: 06 88 06 13 62, www.rent-bike.fr.

BUDGETING FOR YOUR TRIP

The following are approximate prices in euros (€):

Bicycle hire. €12–20 per day, deposit €100–450.

Car hire. €25–60 a day for an economy model, from €180 per week.

Meals and drinks. Breakfast €6–30 depending on category of hotel. In restaurants in the evening expect to pay around €25 for three courses, not including wine, in a budget establishment, €30–40 in a good bistro, €30–70 in a trendy beachside establishment, €80 or more in a top gastronomic restaurant. Coffee €2–4.50; 25cl beer €3–4; sandwich in a café €5–8; salad in a café €10–15.

Museums. Museums in Nice are no longer free. Most now have an entrance fee of €10. Thankfully there are two cost-reducing museum passes available. The 7-day museum pass for €20 admits you to all municipal museums and galleries and The French Riviera Museum Pass, for 1, 2 or 3 days at a cost of €26, €38, €56 respectively, is valid for all municipal museums plus the Chagall Museum and a few museums outside of Nice. Both are available at the Nice Tourist Office at 5 promenade des Anglais, www.nicetourisme.com. The Côte d'Azur Card (www.cotedazur-card.com) is a 3-day card or a 3-day card + Marineland (€45 and 54), which allows you entry to 160 sights in the region, including many museums in Cannes, Nice and Monaco.

Private beach. Day on a sun lounger with parasol €15–40.

C

CAR HIRE (see also Driving)

The major car-hire companies all have branches at Nice airport; most also have branches in Nice (around the train station), Cannes and Monaco. To hire a car, you must have a driving licence (held for at least one year) and a passport. The minimum age varies from 20 to 23. A substantial deposit (refundable) may be required, but most companies swipe your credit card. You will be asked for proof of your local address. Third-party insurance is compulsory. Major car-hire companies include:

Avis: tel: 04 89 98 50 98, www.avis.com
Budget: tel: 04 89 98 50 98, www.budget.com
Europcar: tel: 08 25 81 00 81, www.europcar.com
Hertz: tel: 0825 342 343, www.hertz-europe.com
Rent-a-Car: tel: 04 93 19 07 07, www.rentacar.fr
Elite Rent-a-Car: tel: (Nice) 04 93 39 49 49, (Cannes) 04 93 94 61 00, (Monaco) +377-97 77 17 37, www.eliterent.com. Sports cars and luxury limos with or without a chauffeur.

I'd like to rent a car today/tomorrow **Je voudrais louer une voiture aujourd'hui/demain**
for one day/ the weekend/a week **pour une journée/le week-end/une semaine**

CLIMATE

The French Riviera enjoys a typical Mediterranean climate, with hot, dry summers, mild and wet weather in spring and autumn, and short winters that are usually mild, with occasional cold spells. There are often thunderstorms at night in late August or in September. Here are some average monthly temperatures, but note that peak daytime temperatures can be over 35°C (95°F) in July and August:

		J	F	M	A	M	J	J	A	S	O	N	D
Air	°C	9	9	11	13	17	20	23	22	20	17	12	9
	°F	48	48	52	55	63	68	73	72	68	63	54	48
Sea	°C	13	13	13	15	17	21	24	25	23	20	17	14
	°F	55	55	55	59	63	70	75	77	73	68	63	57

CLOTHING

Cannes and Monaco are the most dressed-up places on the Côte d'Azur, but only the grandest restaurants and casinos require men to wear a jacket and tie (*tenue correcte*). Elsewhere smart casual attire is the norm. Avoid shorts for dining out at night and trainers if you want to get into exclusive nightclubs. In Monaco you are not allowed to walk around the streets in swimwear, and respectable attire is required for religious buildings. Even in summer, a sweater or wrap is useful for cooler evenings, and a waterproof coat or jacket will be needed from October to April.

CRIME AND SAFETY (See also Emergencies and Police)

Inevitably, such a prosperous area attracts petty criminals, and the three cities have some security problems, but incidents of violent crime against visitors are rare. Try not to carry large amounts of cash, never leave valuables in your car, and be on the lookout for pickpockets, especially in crowds. Any loss or theft should be reported immediately to the nearest *commissariat de police*.

D

DRIVING (See also Car Hire)

To take a car into France you'll need a valid driving licence, your car registration papers, insurance coverage and a set of spare bulbs. A red warning triangle and a fluorescent safety waistcoat are obligatory in case of breakdown. Drivers and all passengers (back and front) are required by law to wear seatbelts (where fitted in the back). Children under 10 may not travel in the front of the car other than in appropriate baby seats with the air bag disconnected. Driving with a foreign provisional licence is not permitted. The minimum driving age is 18.

Driving regulations. Drive on the right, pass on the left. In built-up areas, give priority to vehicles coming from the right unless indicated by road markings. At a roundabout, drivers already on the roundabout have priority over those entering it, unless it is marked *priorité à droite*.

Speed limits. When conditions are dry, the limit is 130kmh (80mph) on *autoroutes* (motorways/expressways), 110kmh (70mph) on dual carriageways (divided highways), 90kmh (55mph) on other country roads, 50kmh (30mph) in built-up areas and 30kmh (20mph) in some residential districts. Speed limits are reduced in wet weather. There are speed radars installed on some roads.

Routes and road conditions. The A8 motorway runs west–east across the Côte d'Azur; you can also take the N7 and N98 between Nice and Cannes and the three scenic but twisty Corniches between Nice and Monaco: the Basse (low) Corniche or Corniche Inférieure (N98), Moyenne (middle) Corniche (N7) and the Grande Corniche (D2564). Roads can get very clogged up in summer, especially on Saturdays and around the 14 July and 15 August public holidays.

Parking (*stationnement*). It's wisest to park in an underground car park. If your hotel does not have its own car park, it may have preferential tariffs at a public one. On-street parking is usually on pay-and-display ticket machines. *Stationnement interdit* means 'no parking'. *Sauf riverains* means 'except residents'. Don't leave a car in a *zone piétonne* (pedestrian zone), or where a sign says *stationnement gênant* (parking obstructive), or it may be towed away.

Fuel and oil (*essence; huile*). Unleaded petrol is *essence sans plomb* and diesel is *gasoil*. Most fuel stations are self-service. It's worth filling up on Saturday, since many garages close on Sunday, although large supermarkets often have 24-hour petrol pumps for use with credit cards. Fuel tends to be more expensive on motorways.

E

ELECTRICITY

220-volt, 50-cycle AC is universal. British visitors will need an adaptor (*adaptateur*); American visitors will need a transformer (*transformateur*).

EMBASSIES AND CONSULATES

Most are open from Monday to Friday, from 9 or 10am to 4 or 5pm with an hour or so off for lunch. Most are in Paris or Marseille.

Australia: (Embassy) 4 rue Jean-Rey, 75724 Paris, tel: 01 40 59 33 00, www.france.embassy.gov.au

Canada: (Consulate) 10 rue Lamartine, 06000 Nice, tel: 04 93 92 93 22, www.international.gc.ca

Ireland: (Embassy) 12 avenue Foch, 75116 Paris, tel: 01 44 17 67 00, www.embassyofireland.fr

New Zealand: (Embassy), 103 rue de Grenelle, 75007 Paris, tel: 01 45 01 43 43, www.nzembassy.com/france

South Africa: (Embassy), 59 quai d'Orsay, 75343 Paris, tel: 01 53 59 23 23, www.afriquesud.net

UK: (Consulate) 10 place de la Joliette, 13006 Marseille, tel: 01 44 51 31 00, http://ukinfrance.fco.gov.uk

US: (Consulate) place Varian Fry, 13286 Marseille, tel: 01 43 12 48 85, http://fr.usembassy.gov/embassy-consulates/marseille

EMERGENCIES (see also Health and Police)

In case of an emergency, dial 15 for an ambulance (SAMU), dial **17** for the police (*police-secours*) and **18** for the fire brigade (*sapeurs-pompiers*). Dial **112** from a mobile phone.

G

GETTING THERE (See also Airport)

By car. The 1,200km (750-mile) *autoroute* trip from Calais to Nice (via Reims and bypassing Paris) can take as little as 15 hours. However, *péage* (toll) fees are expensive. For toll estimates and route-planning, see http://fr.mappy.com or www.viamichelin.fr.

By bus. The cheapest way to get to the Riviera is by bus. Eurolines (tel: 0141 862 421, France tel: 08 92 89 90 91, www.eurolines.eu) has services from London to Cannes and Nice.

By train. From the UK, Eurostar trains (tel: 03432 186 186, www.eurostar. co.uk) run from London St Pancras, Ebbsfleet and Ashford International to Lille and Paris Gare du Nord. Services for the South depart from the Gare de Lyon. The high-speed TGV reaches Nice in six hours; some trains also stop at Cannes and Monaco. It is also possible to change trains at Lille. In the UK, tickets can be booked at the International Rail desk at the STA Travel Agency at 52 Grosvenor Gardens, London SW1W 0AU or online at http://en.oui.sncf/en. In France, for SNCF reservations and information, tel: 3635, http://www.oui.sncf. US visitors can visit www.raileurope.com. Enquire about passes and discounts.

By Auto/Train. From June to September, the SNCF operates a daily direct service from Paris Bercy to Nice (tel: 0033 892 35 35 35, http:// autotrain.oui.sncf); less frequent departures off season.

GUIDES AND TOURS

Walking tours. A two-hour guided tour of Vieux Nice in French and English leaves from the main tourist office every Saturday at 9.30am (reserve). The Centre du Patrimoine (14 rue Gilly, Nice, tel: 04 92 00 41 90, www.nice.fr) organises walking tours of Nice's heritage; in English by appointment.

Nice Open Tour. A 90-minute tour of the city on a double-decker bus with the possibility of getting on and off at any of the 12 stops, www. nice.opentour.com.

Boat trips. (see also Iles de Lérins, page 61). Riviera Navigation (tel: +377-92 16 15 15, www.riviera-navigation.com) – hour-long trips along the coast from Monaco's Port Hercule.

Trans Côte d'Azur – trips from Cannes (quai Laubeuf, tel: 04 92 98 71 30) and Nice (quai Lunel, tel: 04 92 00 42 30) to Saint Tropez and Monaco as well as coastal promenades, www.trans-cote-azur.com.

Helicopter tours. Heli Air Monaco (tel: +377-92 05 00 50, www.heliair monaco.com) – 10 and 20-minute tours of the principality.

Tourist mini trains. Sightseeing circuits with commentary in several languages: Trains Touristiques de Nice (www.trainstouristiquesdenice.com) from the promenade des Anglais (near avenue de Verdun) through Vieux

Nice and up Castle Hill; Cannes and the Cinema Tour (tel: 04 92 99 84 22; www.cannes-destination.com) starting from the Cannes tourist office; Monaco Tours (tel: +377-92 05 64 38, www.monacotours.mc) leaving from the Musée Océanographique.

Day trips. Several companies offer half-day and whole-day tours to sights such as Saint-Paul-de-Vence or Gourdon, or further afield to the spectacular Gorges du Verdon or Aix-en-Provence, including Tour Azur (coach or minibus trips from Nice, Cannes and Monaco; tel: 04 93 44 88 77, www.tourazur.com) and Med Tour (minibus tours from Nice; tel: 06 73 82 04 10, www.med-tour.com).

H

HEALTH AND MEDICAL CARE (See also Emergencies)

EU nationals are entitled to use the French Social Security system, which refunds up to 70 percent of medical expenses. To get a refund, British nationals should obtain a European Health Insurance Card before leaving the UK. Available online at www.ehic.org.uk. This is subject to change following Brexit.

Chemists (*pharmacies*) display green crosses. The address of duty chemists open on Sunday and at night is displayed in pharmacies. There is an all-night pharmacy in Nice at 7 rue Masséna.

24-hour casualty departments (*Urgences*):

Nice: Centre Hospitalier Universitaire (CHU) Saint-Roch, 5 rue Pierre Dévoluy, Nice, tel: 04 92 03 77 77.

Monaco: Centre Hospitalier Princesse Grace, 1 avenue Pasteur, Monaco, tel: +377-97 98 97 69.

L

LANGUAGE

Southern French has a warm, pleasing accent, drawing out syllables and placing extra emphasis on the ends of words or sentences. In Vieux

Nice you may see bilingual street names and hear Nissart, an old Occitan Provençal dialect. French is the official language in Monaco, but Italian and English are also widely spoken; you may also come across Monégasque (an Italian dialect).

LGBTQ TRAVELLERS

Nice and Cannes are gay-tolerant cities with several gay bars and clubs; Coco Beach east of Nice's Vieux Port is a popular gay beach. A Gay-friendly Guide to Nice available at www.nicetourisme.com and at the Nice Tourist Office lists gay and gay-friendly bars, hotels, beaches and spas as well as gay events. A list of the French Riviera's gay bars, restaurants, hotels and more is available at http://cotedazur.gaycities. com. There's a lively Gay Pride parade in July in Nice.

M

MAPS

The tourist offices in Nice, Cannes and Monaco can all provide a town street map (un plan), as can most hotels.

MEDIA

Newspapers (journaux). Nice Matin is the principal regional daily; the French nationals (Le Monde, Libération, Le Figaro) are widely available; there is also a Nice version of the free newspaper Métro.

British newspapers and magazines can be found at many newsstands, as can the Paris-based New York Times International Edition and USA Today. There's a particularly wide selection of international newspapers at the Maison de la Presse at 1 place Masséna in Nice. Look out for the English-language glossy magazine Riviera Reporter, which gives an irreverent, insider's view of the region, and the bimonthly RivieraInsider.

Television and radio. France has five main TV channels (TF1, France 2, France 3, Arte, M6), plus the subscription channel Canal+, and numerous cable and satellite channels, often including BBC World or CNN. National radio stations include France Inter (FM 100.2 MHz), France Info (FM 105.7 MHz) and France Musiques (FM 92.2 MHz); RFI (Radio France International) has English-language bulletins; Europe 1 (101.4 MHz) is a good news and general channel; Nostalgie (FM 93.5 MHz) and NRJ (FM 99.2 MHz) are popular music channels; BBC World Service is available at certain times of day on short-wave radio. Monte Carlo's Riviera Radio (106.3 MHz in Monaco and 106.5 in southern France) is an all-English station, broadcasting news, weather, finance and yachting info, and music.

MONEY

Currency (*monnaie*). The unit of currency in both France and Monaco is the euro (€), divided into 100 cents. Banknotes are available in denominations of 500, 200, 100, 50, 20, 10 and 5 euros (many shops will not accept €200 and €500 notes). There are coins for 2 and 1 euros and for 50, 20, 10, 5, 2 and 1 cent.

ATMs. ATMs are plentiful in large cities and are the easiest, and usually cheapest, way of obtaining cash in euros, drawn on either your debit or credit card.

Banks and currency exchange offices (*banques; bureaux de change*). Not all banks have exchange facilities; look for those with a change sign. Big hotels will usually change currency, but the rate is often not favourable.

Credit cards (*cartes de crédit*). Most hotels, restaurants, shops, car-hire firms, motorway toll booths and petrol stations accept major credit cards. There may be a minimum sum (often €15).

Lost and stolen credit cards: Groupement des Cartes Bancaires tel: 0892 70 57 05; American Express tel: 01 47 77 72 00; Diners Club tel: 0820 820 536; Eurocard/MasterCard tel: 0892 705 705; Visa tel: 0800 90 11 79.

I want to change some pounds/dollars. **Je voudrais changer des livres sterling/des dollars.**
Do you accept travellers' cheques/credit cards? **Prenez-vous les chèques de voyage/cartes de crédit?**

O

OPENING TIMES

Shops generally open Mon–Sat 9.30 or 10am to 7pm; bakeries generally open 8am–8pm and may open on Sunday.

Banks usually open Mon–Fri 9am–noon, 2–5pm. Some close on Monday and open on Saturday morning.

Post Nice's main post office, opposite the train station on avenue Thiers, is open Mon–Fri 8am–7pm and Sat 8am–noon; smaller post offices usually open Mon–Fri 9am–noon, 2–5pm, Sat 9am–noon.

Museums usually open 10am–6pm and often close on Monday or Tuesday; smaller ones may close at lunchtime.

P

POLICE

Theft should be reported to the Police Nationale in Nice and Cannes or to the Gendarmerie in smaller towns and rural areas. Monaco has its own, highly visible police force.

Call **17** anywhere in France for police assistance.

Commissariat Central Nice, 1 avenue Maréchal Foch, Nice, tel: 04 92 17 22 22.

Lost property (*objets trouvés*): 42 rue Dabray, Nice, tel: 04 97 13 44 10.

Commissariat de Police, 1 avenue de Grasse, Cannes, tel: 04 93 06 22 22.

Direction de la Sûreté Publique (Police), 3 rue Louis Notari, Monaco; tel: +377-93 15 30 15; lost property +377-93 15 30 18.

POST OFFICES

Post offices display a sign with a stylised bluebird and the words La Poste. In addition to normal mail service, you can buy *télécartes* (phone cards), and receive or send money. If sending letters and small packages, it is quicker to use the automatic stamp machines than to queue for service. Monaco has its own stamps.

PUBLIC HOLIDAYS

In France, banks, public buildings, and most museums and shops close on public holidays, and transport often runs on Sunday schedules.

1 January *Jour de l'An* New Year's Day
March/April *Lundi de Pâques* Easter Monday
1 May *Fête du Travail* Labour Day
8 May *Fête de la Libération* Victory Day (1945)
May *Jeudi de l'Ascension* Ascension Thursday
May/June *Lundi de Pentecôte* Whit Monday
14 July *Fête Nationale* Bastille Day
15 August *Assomption* Assumption
1 November *Toussaint* All Saints' Day
11 November *Anniversaire de l'Armistice* Armistice Day
25 December *Noël* Christmas

In Monaco many museums close for the Monaco Grand Prix in May. Additional holidays in Monaco are:
27 January *Fête de Sainte Dévote* St Devota's Day
May *Fête-Dieu* Corpus Christi
19 November *Fête Nationale* Monaco National Holiday

R

RELIGION

France is a predominantly Roman Catholic country, with minority Protestant, Muslim and Jewish communities. Non Catholic services are called *cultes* and Protestant churches are known as *temples*. Roman Catholicism is the established religion in Monaco. Nice, Cannes and Monaco each have English-speaking Protestant services.

Holy Trinity Anglican Church, 11 rue de la Buffa, Nice, tel: 04 93 87 19 83, www.anglican-nice.com

Holy Trinity Anglican Church, 2–4 avenue du Général Ferrie, Cannes,

tel: 04 93 94 54 61, www.holytrinitycannes.org.
St Paul's Anglican Church Monaco, 22 avenue de Grande-Bretagne,
Monte Carlo, tel: +377-93 30 71 06, www.stpaulsmonaco.com.

T

TELEPHONES

Many public phones only accept *télécartes* (phone cards), which
can be bought at post offices and tobacconists. Specify if you want
a *carte à puce* (works only in phone boxes) or a *carte à code* (works
from any phone).

France uses a 10-digit telephone-number system, whether it is a
local or long-distance call. Numbers on the French Riviera begin with
04. Mobile phone numbers start with 06; special-rate numbers start
with 08, varying from freephone 0800 to premium rate 0892.

When calling France from abroad, dial the French country code 33
and omit the initial 0. The country code for Monaco, which is not on the
10-digit system, is 377. When making overseas calls from France, dial
00 followed by the country code and then the number.

Directory enquiries: various providers, all starting with 118.

Mobile phones. If you are calling a French number from a British-based
mobile in France, dial as if you are a local subscriber. To call from one
British mobile to another, use the international code even if you are
both in France. Some mobiles support Skype, which allows calls for
no or low cost. Most providers offer pre-bought bundles of minutes to
use abroad.

For longer stays, consider buying a French SIM from www.0044.co.uk
or enquire about a *carte prépayée* (pay-as-you-go SIM) in France from
Orange, SFR or Bouygues Télécom. Use WiFi for web browsing as mobile data costs are very expensive.

TIME ZONES

France and Monaco follow Greenwich Mean Time + 1; between March and October the clocks are put forward one hour.

New York	London	**Nice**	Sydney	Auckland
6am	11am	**noon**	8pm	10pm

TIPPING

A 10–15 percent service charge is included in hotel and restaurant bills (to be sure, check for *service compris* on the bill), although rounding up bills with a few coins is appreciated. It is also usual to give hotel porters and filling-station attendants, etc, a few coins, eg: Hotel porter, per bag €1–2, lavatory attendant, €0.50, taxi driver, round up to nearest €5 (optional), tour guide, half-day, €2–5.

TOILETS

There are free toilets in museums and department stores. If using a toilet in a café, it is polite to order at least a coffee at the bar.

TOURIST INFORMATION

Nice: 5 promenade des Anglais, tel: 04 92 14 46 14, www.nicetourisme. com; May Mon–Sat 9am–6pm, Sun 10am–5pm, June–Sept daily 9am–7pm, Oct–Apr Mon–Sat 9am–6pm. Branches at Nice train station (avenue Thiers) and Nice airport (T1).

Cannes: Palais des Festivals, La Croisette, tel: 04 92 99 84 22, www.cannes-destination.fr; daily Mar–Oct 9am–7pm, until 8pm in July and Aug, Nov–Feb 10am–6pm.

Monaco: Direction de Tourismes, 2a boulevard des Moulins, Monte Carlo, tel: +377-92 16 61 16, www.visitmonaco.com; Mon–Sat 9am–7pm, Sun 11am–1pm.

Maison de France (national tourist board) can supply brochures before you go; websites in English on www.france.fr.

Australia: Level 13, 25 Bligh Street, Sydney, NSW 2000, tel: 02 9231

5244.

Canada: 1800 Avenue McGill College, Suite 1010, Montréal, Québec H3A 3J6, tel: 514 288 2026.

UK: Lincoln House, 300 High Holborn, London WC1V 7JH, tel: 0207 061 6600.

US: 825 Third Avenue, 29th floor (entrance on 50th Street), New York, NY 10022, tel: 212 838 745 0967.

TRANSPORT

By bus and tram. Nice has a comprehensive network of urban bus routes and a tramway run by Lignes d'Azur (www.lignesdazur.com), plus five night-bus routes leaving from Promenade des Arts. Single journeys have a flat rate of €1.50, which can be bought on the bus; the same tickets can be used on buses and trams, except for airport express buses Nos 98 and 99 (€6). Useful routes include Nos 17 and 22 for the Musée Matisse in Cimiez, 38 for the Musée des Beaux-Arts, 9, 10 or 23 for the Parc Floral Phoenix.

Buses in Cannes are run by Palm Bus (www.palmbus.fr); most pass the rail and bus stations. Monaco has six public bus routes daily; lines 1 and 2 run between the Casino area (boulevard des Moulins) and Monaco-Ville; individual tickets cost €2.

Regional bus services between Nice, Cannes and Menton are run by RCA (Rapides Côte d'Azur, www.rca.tm.fr). Nice's bus station (*gare routière*) is at 5 boulevard Jean Jaurès.

Trains. The TER regional network links the coastal towns, with branch lines inland from Cannes to Grasse and Nice to Cuneo; you can download timetables on www.ter.sncf.com/paca. Enquire about various categories of tickets for under-26s and OAPs. Eurail passes and Inter-rail cards are valid. See also www.oui.sncf.

Taxis. Nice: Central Taxi Riviera (tel: 04 93 13 78 78); Nice's taxis are notoriously expensive. Cannes: Taxi Cannes (tel: 04 93 99 27 27, www.taxicannes.fr). Monaco: Taxi Monaco Prestige (tel: 08 20 20 98 98).

VISAS AND ENTRY REQUIREMENTS

British visitors need only a passport to enter France, as do nationals of other EU countries and Switzerland. US citizens do not need a visa for stays of up to 90 days. Others should check with the French Embassy in their country for entry requirements.

As France is part of the EU, free exchange of non-duty-free goods for personal use is permitted between France and the UK and the Republic of Ireland. However, duty-free items are still subject to restrictions – check before you go.

WEBSITES AND INTERNET ACCESS

WiFi is now available in many hotels, which means that the number of internet cafés has declined, but there is also access in numerous cafés and at Nice airport. Useful general websites are:

www.nicetourisme.com All things Nice, where to go, what to do.

www.visitmonaco.com The official site with news and information about Monaco and Monte Carlo.

www.beyond.fr Useful information, maps and travel tips concerning Provence.

www.nicerendezvous.com Nice and Côte d'Azur news.

YOUTH HOSTELS

Nice has two youth hostels (*auberges de jeunesse*) affiliated to the Fédération Unie des Auberges de Jeunesse (www.fuaj.org): Les Camélias, 3 rue Spitalieri, tel: 04 93 62 15 54. In the town centre. Mont Boron, route Forestière du Mont Alban, tel: 04 93 89 23 64. On a wooded hill 4km (2.5 miles) from central Nice.

RECOMMENDED HOTELS

Nice and Cannes are among the towns with the largest quantity and variety of accommodation in France, ranging from the grandiose sea-front 'palace hotels' to small family-run places in converted town-houses. Even so, they can be heavily booked during major events and in the high summer. Monaco's hotels are mainly geared to the luxury end of the market, although there are a few small, inexpensive options in La Condamine. The symbols below indicate the average cost of a double room per night in high season, including TVA (VAT), but generally excluding breakfast. An additional tourist tax is charged per person per night, which varies according to the official star rating. All hotels listed have air conditioning and private bathrooms with bath or shower unless indicated. Many hotels also have triple or family rooms, or can add a bed (sometimes for a fee) for a child. The traditional breakfast of coffee, baguette and croissants is increasingly being replaced by a generous buffet. Prices may be lower in winter, but rocket for special events such as the Monaco Grand Prix and the Cannes Film Festival. Look out also for special packages and last-minute deals on the internet. All the hotels listed take major credit cards unless otherwise stated.

€€€€€	over 380 euros
€€€€	260–380 euros
€€€	160–260 euros
€€	90–160 euros
€	below 90 euros

NICE

Hi Hôtel Eco Spa and Beach €€€–€€€€€ *3 avenue des Fleurs, 06000 Nice, tel: 04 97 07 26 26, www.uniqhotels.com.* The hip and colourful Hi Hôtel has become a cult address for design fans, where Matali Crasset's nine different room concepts encourage you to experiment with new ways of living – bath in the middle of the room, pontoon living, high-tech, four-poster bath and operating table bed. There's an organic snack bar and restaurant, and DJs in the bar at weekends. The hotel has a spa and an equally stylish private beach on the promenade des Anglais.

Hôtel Aria €€ *15 avenue Auber, 06000 Nice, tel: 04 93 88 30 69*, www. hotel-aria.fr. This good-value, recently renovated 19th-century hotel overlooks an attractive garden square amid the Belle Epoque and Art Deco buildings of the Musicians' Quarter. Rooms are light and high-ceilinged, in sunny colours.

Hôtel Beau Rivage €€€€€ *24 rue St-François-de-Paule, 06300 Nice, tel: 04 92 47 82 82*, www.hotelnicebeaurivage.com. Located near the Opéra, the hotel where Matisse stayed when he first came to Nice is now a gorgeous exercise in sophisticated minimalism, decorated in natural wood and tones of grey by architect Jean-Michel Wilmotte. TV and internet in every room.

Hôtel du Petit Palais €€ *17 avenue Emile Bieckert, 06000 Nice, tel: 04 93 62 19 11*, www.petitpalaisnice.com. A small, friendly hotel in the pretty ochre-coloured villa on Cimiez hill that once belonged to actor-playwright Sacha Guitry. Some rooms have terraces or balconies with views over Nice and the Baie des Anges, and there's a small paved garden courtyard.

Hôtel Ellington €€€ *25 boulevard Debouchage, 06000 Nice, tel: 04 92 47 79 79*, www.ellington-nice.com. This elegant town centre hotel is a homage to jazz, with an atmospheric 1950s speakeasy-style whisky bar downstairs and photos of jazz musicians in lifts and corridors. Bedrooms vary between black-and-white minimalism and a more traditional Provençal style.

Hôtel Gounod €€ *3 rue Gounod, 06000 Nice, tel: 04 93 16 42 00*, www. gounod-nice.fr. A comfortably refurbished Belle Epoque hotel in the Musicians' Quarter. Guests have access to the pool, spa and gym of the modern but ugly Splendid Hôtel next door.

Hôtel Grimaldi €€–€€€ *15 rue Grimaldi, 06000 Nice, tel: 04 93 16 00 24*, www.le-grimaldi.com. A lovely intimate hotel in the New Town stretching between two Belle Epoque houses on either side of a central courtyard. Helpful staff and comfortable good-sized rooms decorated with colourful neo-Provençal fabrics.

Hôtel Ibis Centre Gare € *14 avenue Thiers, 06000 Nice, tel: 04 93 88 85 55*, www.accorhotels.com. A big, modern branch of the budget chain located near the train station. The 199 rooms offer standard chain decor, but the price is hard to beat, the service efficient and the outdoor swimming pool is a rare plus.

Hôtel La Pérouse €€€€–€€€€€ *11 quai Rauba Capéu, 06300 Nice, tel: 04 93 62 34 63*, www.hotel-la-perouse.com. A luxurious secluded hotel with an astonishing location hidden up the Colline du Château, reached by lift from the quayside, with stunning views over the Baie des Anges. Comfortable traditional rooms, some with a terrace. Swimming pool and an outdoor restaurant open only in summer. Small fitness room.

Hôtel Negresco €€€€€ *37 promenade des Anglais, 06000 Nice, tel: 04 93 16 64 00*, www.hotel-negresco-nice.com. Under its pink-and-green cupola, the Negresco is both Nice's most celebrated hotel and one of its most eccentric, with a mix of elegance and kitsch. Original Old Master paintings, modern sculptures by Nikki de Saint Phalle and a winter garden by Gustave Eiffel mix with gold-plated basins and curiously tacky souvenir shops, while the rooms are furnished with antiques and satin flourishes. There are two restaurants: the haute-cuisine Chantecler and the popular Le 37 Pop. Private beach in front of the hotel.

Hôtel Régence € *21 rue Masséna, 06000 Nice, tel: 04 93 87 75 08*, www.hotelregence.com. This no frills budget hotel is ideally located in central Nice, close to all the attractions. Rooms (€60) are on the small side and simply furnished but clean and tidy.

Hôtel Suisse €€–€€€ *15 quai Rauba Capéu, 06300 Nice, tel: 04 92 17 39 00*, www.hotel-nice-suisse.com. Behind a period facade virtually built into the cliff face of the Colline du Château, the attractive Hôtel Suisse has been stylishly modernised with a different colour scheme on each floor. Most rooms have a sea view and balcony. The gorgeous ground-floor salon includes a tiny cave.

Hôtel Westminster €€€–€€€€€ *27 promenade des Anglais, 06000 Nice,* *tel: 04 92 14 86 86,* www.westminster-nice.com. This venerable pink-stucco seafront hotel has preserved its impressive ground-floor salons and the magnificent open staircase, hung with an interesting collection of historic oil paintings of Vieux Nice. Bedrooms have gradually been redone floor by floor – some in traditional style, the most recent ones in more contemporary soft pearly blues with subtle lighting. Restaurant and bar.

Hôtel Windsor €€–€€€ *11 rue Dalpozzo, 06000 Nice, tel: 04 93 88 59 35,* www.hotelwindsornice.com. From the outside it looks like any 19th-century hotel, but within is a true one-off. Many of the rooms have been individually decorated by internationally renowned contemporary artists, including Robert Barry, Lily van der Stokker, François Morellet, Peter Fend, Jean le Gac, and Ben, who has written all over the walls. Simpler rooms have frescoes or posters. There's a Turkish bath and fitness room, plus outdoor swimming pool and aviary in the lushly planted garden.

Villa La Tour €–€€ *4 rue de la Tour, 06300 Nice, tel: 04 93 80 08 15,* www.villa-la-tour.com. With just 17 rooms in a former monastery, the Villa La Tour is for romantics who want to stay in the Old Town itself. Squashy decrepit sofas in the entrance and individually decorated rooms have a boho charm. You pay slightly more for a view over the Vieux Nice rooftops. No lift.

CANNES

Carlton Intercontinental €€€€€ *58 La Croisette, 06400 Cannes, tel: 04 93 06 40 06,* www.intercontinental.com/cannes. The legendary palace hotel where the jury stays during the film festival has a sweeping Belle Epoque facade and sumptuous suites. It helps to have film-star means as standard rooms can be disappointingly small; avoid those at the rear without sea views. Restaurant, private beach and seasonal beach restaurant, health club and swimming pool.

Grand Hyatt Cannes Hôtel Martinez €€€€–€€€€€ *73 La Croisette,* *06400 Cannes, tel: 04 93 90 12 34,* www.hotel-martinez.com. The splendid facade, acres of marble hallways and grand staircase perpetuate the Art Deco glamour of the 1920s when it was built by Frank Martinez. The 409 bedrooms alternate between classic and Deco style. Two vast penthouse apartments have huge roof terraces, butler service and Turkish baths. Facilities include the Palme d'Or restaurant, a beauty spa and the trendy Zplage in summer.

Hôtel Cavendish €€€–€€€€ *11 boulevard Carnot, 06400 Cannes, tel: 04 97 06 26 00*, www.cavendish-cannes.com. A characterful boutique hotel in an attractive Belle Epoque building on the boulevard that leads towards La Croisette. The comfortable period townhouse style was conceived by decorator Christophe Tollemer as a homage to the English lords who once frequented the coast; some wonderful circular rooms in the corner turret.

Hôtel Château de la Tour €€€–€€€€ *10 avenue Font-de-Veyre, 06150 Cannes La Bocca, tel: 04 93 90 52 52*, www.hotelchateaudelatour.com. On the hill above the Plage du Midi, this is a rare place where you can capture a taste of the aristocratic villa lifestyle – the original wing complete with crenellated turret was built for a countess in the 1880s. Comfortable traditional rooms. The restaurant, open to non-residents, moves out in summer to the exotically planted garden, where there is also an outdoor pool.

Hôtel Molière €€–€€€ *5 rue Molière, 06400 Cannes, tel: 04 93 38 16 16*, www.hotel-moliere.com. Small, well-placed contemporary design hotel with colourful minimalist rooms, at the rear of a long flowery garden; most rooms have balconies.

Hôtel Splendid €€€ *4–6 rue Félix Faure, 06400 Cannes, tel: 04 97 06 22 22*, www.splendid-hotel-cannes.fr. A sparkling white Belle Epoque edifice splendidly placed in the heart of the action, near the port and almost opposite the Palais des Festivals. Rooms have been comfortably updated while retaining period flourishes; breakfast is served on a large sunny terrace.

Le Mistral Hôtel €€ *13 rue des Belges, 06400 Cannes, tel: 04 93 39 91 46*, www.mistral-hotel.com. A great budget discovery in a simple blue-shuttered building just a couple of streets back from the Palais des Festivals, with friendly staff and compact but comfortable rooms in colourful minimalist style. No lift.

MONACO

Hôtel de France €€ *6 rue de la Turbie, La Condamine, 98000 Monaco, tel: +377-93 30 24 64, www.hoteldefrance.mc.* This friendly budget hotel on a side street has an air of the provinces. Rooms are not air-conditioned but have ceiling fans and are clean and tastefully decorated with colourful fabrics. No lift.

Hôtel de Paris €€€€€ *place du Casino, Monte Carlo, 98000 Monaco, tel: +377-98 06 30 00, www.montecarlosbm.com.* The hotel that started it all in 1864 has welcomed anyone who is anyone and is still the grandest place to stay in Monte Carlo, with chandelier-hung lobby, grand staircase and bedrooms and suites that remain firmly in the spirit of another age. The splendid hotel which reopened after meticulous renovation in late 2018, is home to the ever-fashionable Bar Américain, the gourmet Louis XV restaurant and has direct access to Les Thermes Marins spa and gym.

Hôtel Hermitage €€€€€ *square Beaumarchais, Monte Carlo, 98000 Monaco, tel: +377-98 06 40 00, www.montecarlosbm.com.* This Belle Epoque grande dame queens it over Monte Carlo. Already a giant when it opened in the 1880s, it has gone on adding bits ever since, the latest being two new floors and a rooftop putting green, but the winter garden with stained-glass dome by Gustave Eiffel remains the centrepiece. The best rooms have balconies and sea views. Direct access to Les Thermes Marins spa. Excellent Le Vistamar Michelin-starred restaurant of chef Benoit Witz.

Hôtel Métropole Monte Carlo €€€€€ *4 avenue de la Madone, Monte Carlo, 98000 Monaco, tel: +377-93 15 15 15, www.metropole.com.* Behind an astonishing curtain of vegetation, this grand 1880s hotel has been magnificently refurbished by decorator Jacques Garcia. The 141 bedrooms are plush, with lavish fabrics and mahogany and marble bathrooms. There's a cocktail bar, Metropole spa, seawater pool and the Joël Robuchon restaurant.

Hôtel Miramar Cap d'Ail € *126 avenue du 3 Septembre, 06320 Cap d'Ail, tel: 04 93 78 06 60*, http://miramarhotel.fr. Excellent-value hotel just outside Monaco where some of the 25 rooms have balconies with sea views. One of the loveliest beaches on the Riviera, Plage Mala, is a 10-minute walk away.

Hôtel Olympia €€ *17 bis boulevard du Général Leclerc, 06240 Beausoleil, tel: 04 93 78 12 70*, www.olympiahotel.fr. Just across the border into France but only a short walk from the Casino. Corner rooms have attractive bow windows.

Hôtel Port Palace €€€€ *7 avenue Président J-F Kennedy, La Condamine, 98000 Monaco, tel: +377-97 97 90 00*, www.portpalace.com. All 50 rooms and suites have harbour views at this sleek, modern design hotel by the port. There are luxurious leather and marble finishes and floors themed by sea, shells, rock, sun and air. Gym and spa but no pool. The rooftop restaurant serves Mediterranean cuisine.

Le Méridien Beach Plaza €€€€ *22 avenue Princesse Grace, Monte Carlo, 98000 Monaco, tel: +377-93 30 98 80*, www.lemeridien.com. Just east of Larvotto Beach, the huge, modern Méridien Beach has contemporary artworks in the lobby and a 24-hour restaurant where you can watch the chefs cooking in the circular open kitchen. Landscaped outdoor pool, indoor pool and private beach. Two mirror towers provide a high-tech 180° vision of the sea; many of the other guest rooms have balconies with sea views.

Novotel Monte Carlo €€€ *16 boulevard Princesse Charlotte, Monte Carlo, 98000 Monaco, tel: +377-99 99 83 00*, www.accorhotels.com. Built on the former site of Radio Monte Carlo, architect Jean-Michel Wilmotte's building emphasises cream stone, natural wood and glass in a very up-market branch of the modern business chain. There are 218 spacious, minimalist bedrooms, an outdoor pool, a gym and a restaurant with menu conceived by Frédéric Ramos.

EXCURSIONS

Cagnes-sur-mer

Sandton Hôtel Domaine Cocagne €€–€€€€ *30 chemin du Pain de Sucre, 06800 Cagnes-sur-Mer, tel: 04 92 13 57 77, www.sandton.eu.* This lovely hotel, made up of several buildings set in lavender-scented lush parkland overlooking Cagnes-sur-Mer, has minimalist-style accommodation in poolside rooms. Also have family suites (babysitting service available). Closed from November to February.

Vence

Hôtel Diana €€ *79 avenue des Poilus, 06140 Vence, tel: 04 93 58 28 56, www.hotel-diana.fr.* This modern hotel on the edge of Vence's Old Town is tastefully refurbished, some rooms equipped with kitchenettes. A nice place to stay if you're visiting Matisse's Chapelle du Rosaire.

Mougins

Le Mas Candille €€€€€ *boulevard Clément Rebouffel, 06250 Mougins, tel: 04 92 28 43 43, www.lemascandille.com.* Set in wooded grounds on the edge of Mougins village with views across to the Pré-Alpes, this discreetly luxurious hotel has rooms furnished with antiques in an old Provençal farmhouse. There's a poolside restaurant in summer and a gourmet Michelin-starred restaurant all year round with menus by chef Xavier Burelle.

The Estérel

Tiara Miramar Hôtel Beach and Spa €€€–€€€€€ *47 avenue de Miramar, 06590 Théoule-sur-Mer, tel: 04 93 75 05 05, www.miramar-beachspa. tiara-hotels.com.* Located west of Cannes at the foot of the Estérel massif. Comfortable rooms, most with sea views, are all furnished in Provençal prints. The real pluses are the tropical garden, the steps straight down to the sea and a beachside pool.

DICTIONARY

ENGLISH–FRENCH

adj adjective   **adv** adverb   **BE** British English   **n** noun   **prep** preposition   **v** verb

A

abbey l'abbaye
accept v accepter
access v accéder; n accès
accident l'accident
accommodation le logement
account le compte
acetaminophen le paracétamol
acupuncture l'acupuncture
adapter l'adaptateur
address l'adresse
admission l'entrée
after après; **~noon** l'après-midi; **~shave** l'après-rasage
age l'âge
agency l'agence
AIDS Déficience le Syndrome d'immunodéficience acquise
air l'air; **~ conditioning** la climatisation; **~ pump** la pompe à air; **~line** la compagnie aérienne; **~mail** par avion; **~plane** l'avion; **~port** l'aéroport
aisle (plane) le couloir; **~ (theater)** l'allée; **~ seat** le siège couloir
allergic allergique; **~ reaction** la réaction allergique
allow v permettre
alone seul
alter v modifier
aluminum foil le papier aluminium
amazing surprenant
ambulance l'ambulance
American américain
amusement park le parc d'attractions
and et
anemic anémique
anesthesia l'anesthésie
animal l'animal
ankle la cheville
antibiotic l'antibiotique
antiques store l'antiquaire
antiseptic cream la crème antiseptique
anything rien
apartment l'appartement
appendix (body part) l'appendice
appetizer l'entrée
appointment le rendez-vous
arcade la salle de jeux
area code le code régional
arm le bras
aromatherapy l'aromathérapie
around (the corner) au coin
arrivals (airport) les arrivées
arrive v arriver
artery l'artère
arthritis l'arthrite
art l'art
Asian asiatique
aspirin l'aspirine
asthmatic asthmatique
ATM le distributeur automatique de billets; **~ card** la carte de retrait
attack l'attaque
attend v participer
attraction (place) le lieu touristique
attractive beau
Australia l'Australie
Australian australien
automatic automatique; **~ car** la voiture automatique
available disponible

B

baby le bébé; **~ bottle** le biberon; **~ wipe** la lingette pour bébé; **~sitter** le baby-sitter
back (body part) le dos; **~ache** le mal de dos; **~pack** le sac à dos
bag le sac
baggage [BE] le bagage; **~ claim** le retrait des bagages; **~ ticket** l'étiquette
bakery la boulangerie
ballet le ballet
bandage le pansement
bank la banque
bar (place) le bar
barbecue le barbecue
barber le coiffeur pour hommes
baseball le baseball
basket (grocery store) le panier

basketball le basketball
bathroom la salle de bains
battery la pile
battleground le champ de bataille
be v être
beach la plage
beautiful beau
bed le lit; **~ and breakfast** le bed and breakfast
before avant
begin v commencer
beginner le débutant
behind derrière
beige beige
belt la ceinture
berth la couchette
best meilleur
better mieux
bicycle la bicyclette; le vélo
big grand **~ bigger** plus grand
bike route la piste cyclable
bikini le bikini; **~ wax** l'épilation à la cire du maillot
bill (charge) v facturer; **~** n **(invoice)** la facture; **~** n **(money)** la coupure; **~** n **(of sale)** le reçu
bird l'oiseau
birthday l'anniversaire
black noir
bladder la vessie
bland sans goût
blanket la couverture

bleed v saigner
blood le sang; **~ pressure** la tension
blouse le chemisier
blue bleu
board v embarquer; **~ing pass** la carte d'embarquement
boat le bateau
bone l'os
book le livre; **~store** la librairie
boots les bottes
boring ennuyant
botanical garden le jardin botanique
bother v ennuyer
bottle la bouteille; **~ opener** l'ouvre-bouteille
bowl le saladier
box la boîte
boxing match le match de boxe
boy le garçon; **~friend** le petit-ami
bra le soutien-gorge
bracelet le bracelet
brakes (car) les freins
break v **(tooth/bone)** casser
breakdown la panne
breakfast le petit déjeuner
break-in (burglary) l'effraction
breast le sein; **~feed** v allaiter
breathe v respirer
bridge pont
briefs (clothing)

les slips
bring v apporter
British anglais
broken cassé
brooch la broche
broom le balai
brother le frère
brown marron
bug l'insecte
building le bâtiment
burn v brûler
bus le bus; **~ station** la gare routière; **~ stop** l'arrêt de bus; **~ ticket** le ticket de bus; **~ tour** la visite en bus
business les affaires; **~ card** la carte de visite; **~ center** le centre d'affaires; **~ class** la classe affaire; **~ hours** les heures d'ouverture
butcher le boucher
buttocks les fesses
buy v acheter
bye au revoir

C
cabaret le cabaret
cabin la cabine
cable car le téléphérique
café le café
call v appeler; **~ collect** appeler; **~** n l'appel en PCV;
calories les kilocalories
camera l'appareil photo; **~ case** le sac à appareil photo; **~ store** la boutique

photo
camp v camper; **~ing stove** le réchaud; **~site** le camping
can opener le l'ouvre-boîte
Canada le Canada
Canadian canadien
cancel v annuler
candy le bonbon
canned goods les conserves
canyon la gorge
car la voiture; **~ hire [BE]** la voiture de location; **~ park [BE]** le parking; **rental ~** la voiture de location; **~ seat** le siège bébé
carafe la carafe
card la carte; **ATM ~** la carte de retrait; **credit ~** la carte de crédit; **phone ~** le carte de téléphone
carry-on (piece of hand luggage) le bagage à main
cart le chariot
carton le paquet; **~ of**
cigarettes la cartouche de cigarettes
case (amount) le cas
cash v encaisser; **~** n le liquide; **~ advance** l'avance
cashier la caisse
casino le casino
castle le château
cathedral la cathédrale
cave la grotte

CD le CD (disque compact)

cell phone le portable

Celsius Celsius

centimeter le centimètre

certificate le certificat

chair la chaise; **~ lift** le télésiège

change v **(baby)** changer; **~ (money)** échanger; **~** n **(money)** la monnaie;

charcoal le charbon de bois

charge v **(credit card)** payer par carte

charge (cost) le coût

cheap bon marché

cheaper moins cher

check v **(luggage)** enregistrer; **~ (on something)** vérifier; **~** n **(payment)** le chèque; **~-in (hotel/airport)** l'enregistrement; **~ing**

account le compte courant; **~-out (hotel)** quitter la chambre

Cheers! Santé!

chemical toilet les toilettes portables

chemist [BE] la pharmacie

cheque [BE] le chèque

chest (body part) la

poitrine; **~ pain** la douleur à la poitrine

chewing gum le chewing-gum

child l'enfant; **~'s seat** le siège enfant

children's menu le menu enfant

children's portion la portion enfant

chopsticks les baguettes

church l'église

cigar le cigare

cigarette la cigarette

class la classe

classical music la musique classique

clean v nettoyer; **~** adj propre; **~ing product** le produit d'entretien; **~ing supplies** les produits d'entretien

clear v **(on an ATM)** effacer

cliff la falaise

cling film [BE] le cellophane

close v **(shop)** fermer; **~** adv près; **~d** fermé

clothing les vêtements; **~ store** le magasin de vêtements

club le club

coat le manteau

coffee shop le café

coin la pièce

colander la passoire

cold (sickness) le rhume; **~ (tempera-**

ture) froid

colleague le collègue

cologne l'eau de Cologne

color la couleur

comb le peigne

come v venir

complaint la plainte

computer l'ordinateur

concert le concert; **~ hall** la salle de concert

condition (medical) l'état de santé

conditioner l'après-shampooing

condom le préservatif

conference la conférence

confirm v confirmer

congestion la congestion

connect v **(internet)** se connecter

connection (flight) la correspondance; **~ (internet)** la connexion

constipated constipé

consulate le consulat

consultant le consultant

contact v contacter

contact lens les lentilles de contact; **~ solution** la solution pour lentilles de contact

contagious contagieux

convention hall le palais des congrès

conveyor belt le carrousel

cook v cuisiner; **~ing gas** le gaz

cool (temperature) frais

copper le cuivre

corkscrew le tire-bouchon

cost v coûter

cot le lit pliant

cotton le coton

cough v tousser; **~** n la toux

country code le code national

cover charge (bar, club) le droit d'entrée; **~ (restaurant)** le couvert

crash v **(car)** avoir un accident

cream (ointment) la crème

credit card la carte de crédit

crew neck le col rond

crib le berceau

crystal le cristal

cup la tasse

currency la monnaie; **~ exchange** l'échange de monnaie; **~ exchange office** le bureau de change

current account [BE] le compte courant

customs la douane

cut v couper; **~** n **(injury)** la coupure

cute mignon

cycling faire du vélo

D

damage v abîmer; **~d**

endommagé

dance v danser; ~
club la discothèque;
~ing dansant

dangerous dangereux

dark sombre

date (calendar)
la date

day le jour

deaf sourd

debit card la carte
de retrait

deck chair la chaise
longue

declare v déclarer

decline v (**credit
card**) refuser

deeply profondément

degree (temperature)
le degré

delay v retarder

delete v (**computer**)
supprimer

delicatessen la
charcuterie

delicious délicieux

denim jean

dentist le dentiste

denture le dentier

deodorant le
déodorant

department store le
grand magasin

departures (airport)
les départs

deposit v déposer; ~
(**bank**) le dépôt

desert le désert

detergent le
détergent

develop v (**film**)
développer

diabetic diabétique

dial v composer

diamond le diamant

diaper la couche

diarrhea la diarrhée

diesel le gazole

difficult difficile

digital numérique; ~
camera l'appareil
photo numérique;
~ **photo** la photo
numérique

dining room la salle
à manger

dinner le dîner

direction la direction

dirty sale

disabled [BE] handi-
capé; ~ **accessible
[BE]** accessible aux
handicapés

disconnect v (**com-
puter**) déconnecter

discount la réduction

dish (kitchen) la
vaisselle; **~washer**
le lave-vaisselle;
~washing liquid
le détergent pour
lave-vaisselle

display montrer; ~
case la vitrine

disposable jetable;
~ **razor** le rasoir
jetable

dive v plonger;
~ing equipment
l'équipement de
plongée

divorce v divorcer

dizzy avoir des
vertiges

doctor le docteur

doll la poupée

dollar (U.S.) le dollar

domestic national;

~ **flight** le vol
national

door la porte

dormitory le dortoir

double bed le lit
double

downtown (direction)
vers le centre-ville;
~ **area** le centre-
ville

dozen la douzaine

drag lift le remonte-
pentes

**dress (piece of cloth-
ing)** la robe; ~ **code**
la tenue exigée

drink v boire; ~ n la
boisson; ~ **menu** la
carte des boissons

drinking water l'eau
potable

drive v conduire; **~r's
license
number** le numéro de
permis de conduire

drop (medicine) la
goutte

drowsiness la
somnolence

dry cleaner la
teinturerie

dubbed doublé

during pendant

duty (tax) la taxe

duty-free hors taxe

DVD DVD

E

ear l'oreille; **~ache**
l'otite

early tôt

earrings les boucles
d'oreille

east est

easy facile

eat v manger

economy class la
classe économique

elbow le coude

electric outlet la
prise électrique

elevator l'ascenseur

e-mail v envoyer un
mail; ~ n le mail; ~
address l'adresse
mail

emergency l'urgence;
~ **exit** la sortie de
secours

empty v vider

enamel (jewelry)
l'émail

end v finir

English anglais

engrave v graver

enjoy v prendre plaisir

enter v entrer

entertainment le
divertissement

entrance l'entrée

envelope l'enveloppe

equipment
l'équipement

escalators l'escalator

e-ticket le billet
électronique

EU resident le
résident européen

euro l'euro

evening la soirée

excess l'excès

exchange v échanger;
~ n
(**place**) le bureau de
change; ~ **rate** le
taux de change

excursion l'excursion

excuse v excuser

exhausted épuisé
exit v sortir; ~ n la sortie
expensive cher
expert (skill level) l'expert
exposure (film) la pose
express express; ~**bus** le bus direct; ~**train** l'express
extension (phone) le poste
extra extra; ~ **large** très grand
extract v **(tooth)** arracher
eye l'œil
eyebrow wax l'épilation à la cire des sourcils

F

face le visage
facial le soin du visage
family la famille
fan (appliance) le ventilateur; ~ **(souvenir)** l'éventail
far loin
farm la ferme
far-sighted presbyte
fast vite; ~ **food** le fast food
faster plus vite
fat free 0% de matières grasses
father le père
fax v envoyer un fax; ~ n le fax; ~ **number** le numéro de fax
feed v nourrir

ferry le ferry
fever la fièvre
field (sports) le terrain de sport
fill v faire le plein
fill v **out (form)** remplir
filling (tooth) le plombage
film (camera) la pellicule
fine (fee for breaking law) la contravention
finger le doigt; ~**nail** l'ongle
fire le feu; ~ **department** les pompiers; ~ **door** la porte coupe-feu
first premier; ~ **class** la première classe
fitting room la cabine d'essayage
fix v **(repair)** réparer
flashlight la lampe torche
flat tire [tyre BE] le pneu crevé
flight le vol
floor le sol
flower la fleur
folk music la musique folklorique
food la nourriture
foot le pied
football [BE] le football; ~ **game [BE]** le match de football
for pour
forecast la météo
forest la forêt
fork la fourchette

form le formulaire
formula (baby) le lait pour bébés
fort le fort
fountain la fontaine
France la France
free libre
freezer le congélateur
French français
fresh frais
friend l'ami
frying pan la poêle
full-service le service complet
full-time le temps plein

G

game le match
garage le garage
garbage bag le sac poubelle
gas l'essence; ~ **station** la station service
gate (airport) la porte
gay gay; ~ **bar** le bar gay; ~ **club** le club gay
gel (hair) le gel
get off v **(a train, bus, subway)** descendre
get to v **aller**
gift le cadeau; ~ **shop** la boutique cadeaux
girl la fille; ~**friend** la petite-amie
give v donner
glass le verre;
glasses les lunettes
go v **(somewhere)** aller

gold l'or
golf course le terrain de golf
golf tournament le tournoi de golf
good adj bon; ~ n le produit; ~ **afternoon** bon après-midi; ~ **evening** bonsoir; ~ morning bonjour; ~**bye** au revoir
goods les produits
gram le gramme
grandchild les petits-enfants
grandparent les grands-parents
gray gris
green vert
grocery store le magasin de fruits et légumes
ground floor le rez-de-chaussée
groundcloth le tapis de sol
groundsheet le drap du dessous
group le groupe
guide le guide; ~ **book** le guide; ~ **dog** le chien d'aveugle
gym la gym
gynecologist le gynécologue

H

hair les cheveux; dryer le sèche-cheveux d'étudiant; ~ **salon** le coiffeur; ~**brush** la brosse; ~**cut** la coupe de cheveux; ~**spray** la laque; **~style** le style de coiffure; **~stylist** le coiffeur

half la moitié; **~ hour** la demi-heure **~-kilo** le demi-kilo

hammer le marteau

hand la main; **~ luggage [BE]** le bagage à main; **~bag [BE]** le sac à main

handicapped l'handicapé; **~-accessible** accessible aux **handicapés**

hangover la gueule de bois

happy heureux

hat le chapeau

have v avoir

head (body part) la tête; **~ache** le mal de tête; **~phones** les écouteurs

health la santé; **~ food store** le magasin de produits diététiques

heart le cœur; **~ condition** le problème cardiaque

heat le chauffage; **~er** le chauffage

hectare l'hectare

hello bonjour

helmet le casque

help v aider; **~** n l'aide

here ici

hi salut

high haut; **~chair** la chaise haute; **~-heeled shoes**

les chaussures à talons aiguilles; **~way** l'autoroute

hiking boots les chaussures de marche

hill la colline

hire v [BE] louer; **~ car [BE]** la voiture de location

hitchhike v faire de l'auto-stop

hockey le hockey

holiday [BE] les vacances

horsetrack le champ de course

hospital l'hôpital

hostel l'auberge de jeunesse

hot (spicy) épicé; **~ (temperature)** chaud; **~ spring** la source chaude; **~ water** l'eau chaude

hotel l'hôtel

hour l'heure

house la maison; **~hold goods** les produits ménagers; **~keeping service** le service d'entretien

how comment; **~ much** combien

hug v enlacer

hungry faim

hurt la douleur

husband le mari

I

ibuprofen l'ibuprofène

ice la glace; **~**

hockey le hockey sur glace

icy glacé

identification l'identification

ill malade

in dans

include v inclure

indoor pool la piscine intérieure

inexpensive pas cher

infected infecté

information (phone) les renseignements; **~ desk** le bureau des renseignements

insect l'insecte; **~ bite** la piqure d'insecte; **~ repellent** la lotion anti-insectes

insert v insérer

insomnia l'insomnie

instant message le message **instantané**

insulin l'insuline

insurance l'assurance; **~ card** la carte d'assurance; **~ company** la compagnie d'assurance

interesting intéressant

intermediate le niveau intermédiaire

international (airport area) l'international (terminal); **~ flight** le vol international;

~ student card la carte internationale d'étudiant

internet l'internet; **~ cafe** le cyber café; **~ service** le service internet

interpreter l'interprète

intersection l'intersection

intestine l'intestin

introduce v présenter

invoice [BE] la facture

Ireland l'Irlande

Irish irlandais

iron v repasser; **~** n **(clothes)** le fer à repasser

Italian italien

J

jacket la veste

jar le pot

jaw la mâchoire

jazz le jazz; **~ club** le club de jazz

jeans le jean

jet ski le jet ski

jeweler la bijouterie

jewelry le bijou

join v joindre

joint (body part) l'articulation

K

key la clé; **~ card** la carte de la chambre; **~ ring** la chaîne

kiddie pool la pataugeoire

kidney (body part) le rein

kilo le kilo; **~gram** le kilogramme; **~meter** le kilomètre
kiss v embrasser
kitchen la cuisine; **~ foil** [BE] le papier aluminium
knee le genou
knife le couteau

L

lace la dentelle
lactose intolerant allergique au lactose
lake le lac
large grand
larger plus grand
last dernier
late (time) tard
later plus tard
laundromat la laverie automatique
laundry la lessive; **~ facility** la buanderie; **~ service** le service de nettoyage
lawyer l'avocat
leather le cuir
leave v partir
left (direction) à gauche
leg la jambe
lens le verre
less moins
lesson la leçon
letter la lettre
library la bibliothèque
life jacket le gilet de sauvetage
lifeguard le secouriste
lift [BE] l'ascenseur;

~ pass le forfait
light (cigarette) v allumer; **~ adj (overhead)** blond; **~bulb** l'ampoule
lighter le briquet
like v aimer
line (train) la ligne
linen le lin
lip les lèvres
liquor store le marchand de vins et de spiritueux
liter le litre
little adv peu; **~ adj** petit
live v vivre
liver (body part) le foie
loafers les mocassins
local du quartier
lock v fermer; **~ n** le cadenas; **~er** la consigne
log off (computer) terminer une session
log on (computer) ouvrir une session
long long; **~ sleeves** les manches longues; **~-sighted** [BE] presbyte
look v regarder
lose v (something) perdre
lost perdu; **~ and found** les objets trouvés
lotion la crème
louder plus fort
love v (someone) aimer; **~ n** amour
low bas

luggage le bagage; **~ cart** le chariot; **~ locker** la consigne; **~ ticket** le retrait des bagages
lunch le déjeuner
lung le poumon

M

magazine le magazine
magnificent magnifique
mail le courrier; **~box** la boîte-à-lettres
main attraction la principale attraction touristique
main course le plat principal
mall le centre commercial
man l'homme
manager le responsable
manicure la manucure
manual car la voiture manuelle
map la carte
market le marché
married marié
marry v se marier
mass (church service) la messe
massage le massage
match le match
meal le repas
measure v (someone) mesurer
measuring cup la mesure
measuring spoon la cuillère à doser

mechanic le mécanicien
medicine le médicament
medium (size) moyen
meet v (someone) rencontrer
meeting la réunion; **~ room** la salle de réunion
membership card la carte de membre
memorial (place) le lieu commémoratif
memory card la carte mémoire mend v raccourcir
menstrual cramp les règles douloureuses
menu la carte
message le message
meter (parking) l'horodateur
microwave le micro-onde
midday [BE] midi
midnight minuit
mileage le kilométrage
mini-bar le mini bar
minute la minute
missing disparu
mistake l'erreur
mobile home le mobile home
mobile phone [BE] le portable
mobility la mobilité
money l'argent
month le mois
mop la serpillière
moped la mobylette
more plus
morning le matin

mosque la mosquée
mother la mère
motion sickness (air) le mal de l'air; **~ (sea)** le mal de mer
motor boat le bateau à moteur
motorcycle la mobylette
motorway [BE] l'autoroute
mountain la montagne mousse la mousse
mouth la bouche
movie le film; **~ theater** le cinéma
mug v attaquer
muscle le muscle
museum le musée
music la musique; **~ store** le disquaire

N

nail file la lime á ongle
nail salon l'onglerie
name le nom
napkin la serviette
nappies [BE] les couches
nationality la nationalité
nature preserve la réserve naturelle
nausea la nausée
near près; **~by** près de; **~sighted** myope
neck le cou
necklace le collier
need v avoir besoin
newspaper le journal

newsstand le kiosque à journaux
next suivant
nice bien
night la nuit
nightclub le night club
no non
non-alcoholic non alcoolisé
non-smoking non fumeur
noon midi
north nord
nose le nez
note [BE] la coupure
nothing rien
notify v informer
novice (skill level) novice
now maintenant
number le nombre; le numéro
nurse l'infirmier

O

office le bureau; **~ hours** les heures d'ouverture
off-licence [BE] le marchand de vins et de spiritueux
oil l'huile
OK d'accord
old vieux
on the corner au coin
once une fois
one un; **~-way (ticket)** l'aller simple; **~-way street** le sens unique
only seulement
open v ouvrir; **~** adj ouvert

opera l'opéra; **~ house** l'opéra
opposite le contraire
optician l'opticien
orange (color) orange
orchestra l'orchestre
order v commander
outdoor pool la piscine extérieure
outside dehors
over-the-counter (medication) sans ordonnance
overlook (scenic place) le point d'observation
overnight de nuit
oxygen treatment le soin à l'oxygène

P

pacifier la tétine
pack v faire les bagages
package le colis
pad [BE] la serviette hygiénique
pain la douleur
pajamas le pyjama
palace le palais
panties les culottes
pants le pantalon
pantyhose le collant
paper le papier; **~ towel** la serviette en papier
paracetamol [BE] le paracétamol
park v se garer; **~** n le parc; **~ing garage** le garage; **~ing lot** le parking
part (for car) la

pièce; ~-time le temps partiel
pass through v passer
passenger le passager
passport le passeport; **~ control** le contrôle de passeport
password le mot de passe
pastry shop la pâtisserie
path le chemin
pay v payer; **~ phone** le téléphone public
peak (of a mountain) le sommet
pearl la perle
pedestrian le piéton
pediatrician le pédiatre
pedicure la pédicure
pen le stylo
penicillin la pénicilline
penis le pénis
per par; **~ day** par jour; **~ hour** par heure; **~ night** par nuit; **~ week** par semaine
perfume le parfum
period (menstrual) les règles; **~ (of time)** la période
permit v permettre
personal identification number (PIN) le code secret
petite menue
petrol [BE] le l'essence; **~ station**

[BE] la station service
pewter l'étain
pharmacy la pharmacie
phone v téléphoner; ~ n le téléphoner; ~ **call** l'appel; ~ **card** la carte de téléphone; ~ **number** le numéro de téléphone
photo la photo; ~**copy** la photocopie; ~**graphy** la photographie
pick up v (something) prendre
picnic area l'aire de pique-nique
piece le morceau
Pill (birth control) la pilule
pillow l'oreiller
pink rose
piste [BE] la piste; ~ **map [BE]** la carte des pistes
pizzeria la pizzeria
place v (a bet) parier
plane l'avion
plastic wrap le cellophane
plate l'assiette
platform le quai
platinum platine
play v jouer; ~ n (theater) la pièce ~**ground** l'aire de jeux ~**pen** le parc
please s'il vous plaît
pleasure le plaisir
plunger le déboucheur de toilettes

plus size grande taille
pocket la poche
poison le poison
poles (skiing) les bâtons
police la police; ~ **report** le rapport de police; ~ **station** le commissariat de police
pond l'étang
pool la piscine
pop music la pop musique
portion la portion
post [BE] le courrier; ~ **office** le bureau de poste; ~**box [BE]** la boîte-à-lettres; ~**card** la carte postale
pot la casserole
pottery la poterie
pound (British sterling) la livre sterling
pregnant enceinte
prescribe v prescrire
prescription l'ordonnance
press v (clothing) repasser
price le prix
print v imprimer
problem le problème
produce v produire; ~ **store** le marchand de fruits et légumes
prohibit v interdire
pronounce v prononcer
public public
pull v (door sign)

tirer
purple pourpre
purse le sac
push v (door sign) pousser
pushchair [BE] la poussette

Q

quality la qualité
question la question
quiet le silence; le calme

R

racetrack la piste de courses
racket (sports) la raquette
railway station [BE] la gare
rain la pluie; ~**coat** l'imperméable; ~**forest** la forêt vierge
rainy pluvieux
rap (music) le rap
rape v violer; ~ n le viol
rash l'irritation cutanée
razor blade la lame de rasoir
reach v atteindre
ready prêt
real vrai
receipt le reçu
receive v recevoir
reception la réception
recharge v recharger
recommend v recommander
recommendation la

recommandation
recycling les ordures à recycler
red rouge
refrigerator le réfrigérateur
region la région
registered mail le courrier recommandé
regular ordinaire
relationship la relation
rent v louer; ~**al car** la voiture de location
repair v réparer
repeat v répéter
reservation la réservation; ~ **desk** le bureau de réservation
reserve v réserver
restaurant le restaurant
restroom les toilettes
retired v prendre sa retraite
return v (something) rendre; ~ n **[BE]** l'aller-retour
rib (body part) la côte
right (direction) à droite; ~ **of way** le droit de passage
ring la bague
river la rivière
road map la carte routière
rob v voler
romantic romantique
room la pièce; ~ **key** la clé; ~ **service** le service de chambre

round-trip l'aller-retour
route la route
rowboat la barque
rubbish [BE] les poubelles; **~ bag [BE]** le sac poubelle
rugby le rugby
ruins les ruines

S

sad triste
safe adj en sécurité; **~** n le coffre-fort
sales tax la TVA
same le même
sandals les sandales
sanitary napkin la serviette hygiénique
saucepan la casserole
sauna le sauna
save v **(computer)** sauvegarder
savings (account) le compte épargne
scanner scanner
scarf l'écharpe
schedule v prévoir; **~** n l'horaire
science la science
scissors les ciseaux
sea la mer
seat le siège
security la sécurité
see v voir
self-service le self-service
sell v vendre
seminar le séminaire
send v envoyer
senior citizens les seniors

separated (marriage) séparés
serious sérieux
service (in a restaurant) le service
sexually transmitted disease (STD) les maladies sexuellement transmissibles
shampoo le shampooing
sharp tranchant
shaving cream la mousse à raser
sheet le drap
shirt la chemise
ship v envoyer
shoe store le magasin de chaussures
shoes les chaussures
shop v faire des achats
shopping les courses; **~ area** le quartier des magasins; **~ centre [BE]** le centre commercial; **~ mall** le centre commercial
short court; **~-sighted[BE]** myope; **~ sleeves** les manches courtes; **~s** le short
shoulder l'épaule
show v montrer
shower la douche
shrine le lieu saint
sick malade
side dish l'accompagnement
side effect l'effet secondaire

sightseeing le tourisme; **~** la visite touristique
sign v signer
silk la soie
single (unmarried) adj célibataire; n **~ bed** le lit une place; **~ prints** le tirage unique; **~ room** la chambre simple
sink l'évier
sister la sœur
sit v s'asseoir
size la taille
ski v skier; **~** n le ski; **~ lift** le télésiège
skin la peau
skirt la jupe
sleep v dormir
sleeper car le wagon couchette
sleeping bag le sac de couchage
sleeping car [BE] le wagon couchette
slice la tranche
slippers les chaussons
slower plus lent
slowly lentement
small petit
smaller plus petit
smoke v fumer
smoking (area) la zone fumeur
snack bar le bar
sneakers les tennis
snorkeling equipment l'équipement de plongée
snowboard le snowboard

snowshoe la chaussure de ski
snowy neigeux
soap le savon
soccer le football; **~ game** le match de football
sock la chaussette
soother [BE] la tétine
sore throat le mal de gorge
sorry désolé
south sud
souvenir le souvenir; **~ store** le magasin de souvenirs
spa le spa
spatula la spatule
speak v parler
special (food) la spécialité; le plat typique
specialist (doctor) le spécialiste
specimen l'échantillon
speed (velocity) la vitesse
spell v épeler
spicy épicé
spine (body part) la colonne vertébrale
spoon la cuillère
sporting goods store le magasin de sport
sports le sport; **~ massage** le massage sportif
sprain l'entorse
stadium le stade
stairs les escaliers
stamp v **(a ticket)** timbrer; **~** n **(post-**

age) le timbre
start v **(a car)** démarrer; v **(to begin)** commencer
starter [BE] l'entrée
station la station; **~ wagon** le break; **bus ~** la gare routière; **gas ~** la station service; **muster ~ [BE]** la salle d'attente; **petrol ~ [BE]** la station service; **subway ~** la station de métro; **train ~** la gare
statue la statue
stay v rester
steal v voler
steep escarpé
sterling silver l'argent fin
sting la piqûre
stolen volé
stomach l'estomac; **~ache** les maux de ventre
stop v arrêter; **~** n l'arrêt
store directory le plan du magasin
stove la gazinière
straight droit
strange étrange
stream le ruisseau
stroller la poussette
student l'étudiant
study v étudier
stunning stupéfiant
subtitle subtil
subway le métro; **~ station** la station de métro
suit le costume;

~case la valise
sun le soleil; **~ block** l'écran solaire; **~burn** le coup de soleil; **~glasses** les lunettes de soleil
sunny ensoleillé
sunscreen la crème solaire
sunstroke l'insolation
super (fuel) le super; **~market** le supermarché; **~vision** la supervision
surfboard le surf
swallow v avaler
sweater le pull
sweatshirt le sweat-shirt
sweet (taste) sucré
sweets [BE] les bonbons
swell v gonfler
swim v nager
swimsuit le maillot de bain
symbol (keyboard) le symbole
synagogue la synagogue

T

table la table
tablet (medicine) le cachet
take v prendre
take away [BE] à emporter
tampon le tampon
taste v goûter
taxi le taxi
team l'équipe

teaspoon la cuillère à café
telephone le téléphone
temple (religious) le temple
temporary temporaire
tennis le tennis
tent la tente; **~ peg** le piquet; **~ pole** le pilier
terminal (airport) le terminal
terracotta la terre cuite
terrible terrible
text v **(send a message)** écrire; **~** n **(message)** le texte
thank v remercier; **~ you** merci
that ça/cela
theater le théâtre
theft le vol
there là
thief le voleur
thigh la cuisse
thirsty soif
this ceci
throat la gorge
ticket le billet; **~ office** la billetterie
tie (clothing) la cravate
time le temps; **~table [BE]** les horaires
tire [tyre BE] le pneu
tired fatigué
tissues les Kleenex
to go aller
tobacconist le tabac

today aujourd'hui
toe l'orteil; **~nail** l'ongle
toilet [BE] les toilettes; **~ paper** le papier toilette
tomorrow demain
tongue la langue
tonight ce soir
too trop
tooth la dent; **~paste** le dentifrice
total (amount) le total
tough (food) dur
tour la visite
tourist le touriste; **~ information office** le syndicat d'initiative
tow truck la dépanneuse
towel la serviette
tower la tour
town la ville; **~ hall** la mairie; **~ map** la carte de la ville; **~ square** le centre ville
toy le jouet; **~ store** le magasin de jouets
track (train) le quai
traditional traditionnel
traffic light le feu tricolore
trail la piste; **~ map** la carte des pistes
trailer la remorque
train le train; **~ station** la gare
translate v traduire
trash les poubelles

travel v voyager; **~ agency** l'agence de voyage; **~ sickness** le mal des transports; **~er's check [cheque BE]** le chèque de voyages
tree l'arbre
trim (hair cut) v égaliser
trip le voyage
trolley [BE] le chariot
trousers [BE] le pantalon
T-shirt le t-shirt
turn off v (lights) éteindre
turn on v (lights) allumer
TV la télé
type v taper

U

ugly laid
umbrella le parapluie
unattended sans surveillance
unbranded medication [BE] le médicament générique
unconscious inconscient
underground [BE] le métro; **~ station [BE]** la station de métro
underpants [BE] les slips
understand v comprendre

underwear les sous-vêtements
United Kingdom (U.K.) le Royaume Uni
United States (U.S.) les États-Unis
university l'université
unleaded (gas) sans plomb
upper supérieur
urgent urgent
use v utiliser
username le nom de l'utilisateur
utensil l'ustensile

V

vacancy libre
vacation les vacances
vaccination la vaccination
vacuum cleaner l'aspirateur
vagina le vagin
vaginal infection l'infection vaginale
valid valide
valley la vallée
valuable précieux
value la valeur
VAT [BE] la TVA
vegetarian végétarien
vehicle registration la carte grise
viewpoint [BE] le point d'observation
village le village
vineyard le vignoble
visit v visiter; **~ing hours** les heures de visite
visually impaired le malvoyant
vitamin la vitamine

V-neck le col en V
volleyball game le match de volleyball
vomit v vomir

W

wait v attendre; **~** n l'attente
waiter le serveur
waiting room la salle d'attente
waitress la serveuse
wake v réveiller; **~-up call** n l'appel réveil
walk v marcher; **~** n la promenade; **~ing route** le chemin de randonnée
wall clock la pendule
wallet le portefeuille
warm (something) v réchauffer **~** adj **(temperature)** chaud
washing machine la machine à laver
watch la montre
water skis les skis nautiques
waterfall la cascade
weather le temps
week la semaine; **~-week-end** le week-end
weekly hebdomadaire
welcome v accueillir
well-rested bien reposé
west ouest
what quoi
wheelchair la chaise roulante; **~ ramp** la rampe d'accès

when quand
where où
white blanc; **~ gold** l'or blanc
who qui
widow le veuf
wife l'épouse
window la fenêtre; **~ case** le chambranle
windsurfer le véliplanchiste
wine list la carte des vins
wireless internet l'accès Wi-Fi
wireless phone le portable
with avec
withdraw v retirer
withdrawal (bank) le retrait
without sans
woman la femme
wool la laine
work v travailler
wrap v emballer
wrist le poignet
write v écrire

Y

year l'année
yellow jaune; **~ gold** l'or jaune
yes oui
yesterday hier
you're welcome de rien
young jeune
youth hostel l'auberge de jeunesse

Z

zoo le zoo

FRENCH-ENGLISH

A

à droite right (direction)

à gauche left (direction)

l'abbaye abbey

abîmer v damage

accéder v access

accepter v accept

l'accès Wi-Fi wireless internet

accessible aux handicapés handicapped- [disabled- BE] accessible

l'accident accident

l'accompagnement side dish

d'accord OK

accueillir v welcome

acheter v buy

l'acupuncture acupuncture

l'adaptateur adapter

l'addition bill (check)

l'adresse address; ~ **mail** e-mail address

l'aéroport airport

les affaires business

l'âge age

l'agence agency; ~ **de voyage** travel agency

l'aide n help

aider v help

aimer v like (someone); ~ v love (someone)

l'aire de jeux playground; ~ **de sport** field (sports)

l'aire de pique-nique picnic area

allaiter v breastfeed

l'allée aisle (theater)

aller v go (somewhere)

l'aller simple one-way (ticket)

allergique allergic; ~ **au lactose** lactose intolerant

l'aller-retour round-trip [return BE]

allumer v light (cigarette); ~ v turn on (lights)

l'ambulance ambulance

américain American

l'ami friend

amour n love

l'ampoule lightbulb

anémique anemic

l'anesthésie anesthesia

anglais British; English

l'animal animal

l'année year

l'anniversaire birthday

annuler v cancel

l'antibiotique antibiotic

l'antiquaire antique store

l'appareil photo camera; ~ **numérique** digital camera

l'appartement apartment

l'appel phone call

appeler v call

l'appendice appendix (body part)

apporter v bring

après after

l'après after; ~**-midi** afternoon; ~**-rasage** aftershave; ~**-shampooing** conditioner

l'arbre tree

la salle de jeux arcade

l'argent money; ~ **fin** sterling silver

l'aromathérapie aromatherapy

arracher v extract (tooth)

l'arrêt n stop; ~ **de bus** bus stop

arrêter v stop

les arrivées arrivals (airport)

arriver v arrive

l'art arts

l'artère artery

l'arthrite arthritis

l'articulation joint (body part)

l'ascenseur elevator [lift BE]

asiatique Asian

l'aspirateur vacuum cleaner

l'aspirine aspirin

l'assiette plate

l'assurance insurance

asthmatique asthmatic

l'attaque attack

attaquer v mug

atteindre v reach

attendre v wait

l'attente n wait

au coin on/around the corner

au revoir goodbye

l'auberge de jeunesse youth hostel

aujourd'hui today

l'Australie Australia

australien Australian

automatique automatic

l'autoroute highway [motorway BE]

avaler v swallow

l'avance cash advance

avant before

avec with

l'avion airplane

l'avocat lawyer

avoir v have; ~ **besoin** v need; ~ **des vertiges** dizzy; ~ **la nausée** nauseous; ~ **un accident** v crash (car)

B

le baby-sitter babysitter

le bagage à main carry-on [piece of hand luggage BE]

le bagage luggage [baggage BE]

la bague ring

les baguettes chopsticks

le balai broom

le ballet ballet

la banque bank

le bar bar (place), snack bar; **~ gay** gay bar

le barbecue barbecue

la barque rowboat

bas low

le baseball baseball

le basketball basketball

le bateau boat; **~ à moteur** motor boat

le bâtiment building

les bâtons poles (skiing)

beau attractive, beautiful

le bébé baby

le bed and breakfast bed and breakfast

beige beige

belle pretty

le berceau crib

le biberon baby bottle

la bibliothèque library

la bicyclette bicycle

bien well; **~ reposé** well-rested

le bijou jewelry

la bijouterie jeweler

le bikini bikini

la billeterie ticket office; **~ électronique** e-ticket

blanc white

bleu blue

boire v drink

la boisson n drink

la boîte box; **~-à-lettres** mailbox [postbox BE]

bon adj good; **~ après-midi** good afternoon; **~marché** cheap

le bonbon candy [sweet BE]

bonjour hello, good morning

bonsoir good evening

les bottes boots

la bouche mouth

le boucher butcher

les boucles d'oreille earrings

la boulangerie bakery

la bouteille bottle

la boutique photo camera store

le bracelet bracelet

le bras arm

le briquet lighter

la broche brooch

la brosse hairbrush

brûler v burn

la buanderie laundry facility

le bureau office; **~ de change** currency exchange office; **~ de poste** post office; **~ des renseignements** information desk; **~ de réservation** reservation desk

le bus bus; **~ direct** express bus

C

ça that

le cabaret cabaret

la cabine cabin; **~ d'essayage** fitting [changing BE] room

le cachet tablet (medicine)

le cadeau gift

le cadenas n lock

le café café, coffee shop

la caisse cashier

les kilocalories calories

camper v camp

le camping campsite

le Canada Canada

canadien Canadian

la carafe carafe

le carrousel conveyor belt

la carte map, card; **~ d'assurance** insurance card; **~ des boissons** drink menu; **~ de la chambre** key card; **~ de crédit** credit card; **~ d'embarquement** boarding pass; **~ internationale d'étudiant** international student card; **~ grise** vehicle registration; **~ de membre** membership card; **~ mémoire** memory card; **~ des pistes** trail [piste BE] map; **~ postale** postcard; **~ de retrait** ATM/debit card; **~ routière** road map; **~ de téléphone** phone card; **~ de la ville** town map; **~ de visite** business card

la carte des vins wine list

la cartouche (de cigarettes) carton (of cigarettes)

le cas case (amount)

la cascade waterfall

le casino casino

le casque helmet

cassé broken

casser v break (tooth, bone)

la casserole pot, saucepan

la cathédrale cathedral

la cave cave, cellar (wine)

le CD (disque compact) CD

ce soir tonight

ceci this

la ceinture belt

cela that

célibataire single (unmarried)

le cellophane plastic wrap [cling film BE]

Celsius Celsius

le centimètre centimeter

centre center; **~ commercial** shopping mall [centre BE]; **~ d'affaires** business center; **~ ville** town square; **~-ville** downtown area

le certificat certificate

la chaîne key ring, chain

la chaise chair; **~ haute** highchair; **~ longue** deck chair; **~ roulante** wheelchair

le chambranle display window/case

la chambre simple single room

le champ field; **~ de bataille** battleground; **~ la piste de course** horsetrack

le change n exchange (place)

changer v change (baby)

le chapeau hat

le charbon de bois charcoal

la charcuterie delicatessen

le chariot cart [trolley BE]

le château castle

chaud hot, warm (temperature)

le chauffage heat (indoor)

le chauffage heater

la chaussette sock

les chaussons slippers

les chaussures shoes; **~ de ski** snowshoes; **~ à talons aiguilles** high-heeled shoes; **~ de marche** hiking boots; **~ plates** flat shoes

le chemin trail, path; **~ de randonnée** walking route

la chemise shirt

le chemisier blouse

le chèque n check [cheque BE] (payment); **~ de voyages** traveler's check [cheque BE]

cher expensive

les cheveux hair

la cheville ankle

le chewing-gum chewing gum

le chien d'aveugle guide dog

chinois Chinese

le cigare cigar

la cigarette cigarette

le cinéma movie theater

les ciseaux scissors

la classe class; **~ affaire** business class; **~ économique** economy

class

la clé key

la climatisation air conditioning

le club club; **~ gay** gay club; **~ de jazz** jazz club

le code n **~ national** country code; **~ régional** area code; **~ secret** personal identification number (PIN)

le cœur heart

le coffre-fort safe (receptacle)

le coiffeur hair salon

le coiffeur pour hommes barber

le col rond crew neck

le col en V V-neck

le colis package

le collègue colleague

le collier necklace

la colline hill

la colonne vertébrale spine (body part)

combien how much

commander v order

commencer v begin

comment how

le commissariat de police police station

la compagnie aérienne airline

la compagnie d'assurance insurance company

composer v dial

comprendre v understand

le compte account; **~ courant** checking

[current BE] account; **~ épargne** savings account

le concert concert

conduire v drive

la conférence conference

confirmer v confirm

le congélateur freezer

la congestion congestion

se connecter v connect (internet)

la connexion connection (internet, telephone)

les conserves canned goods

la consigne luggage locker

la consigne locker

constipé constipated

le consulat consulate

le consultant consultant

contacter v contact

contagieux contagious

le contraire opposite

la contravention fine (fee for breaking law)

le contrôle de passeport passport control

la correspondance change (buses); **~ connection** (flight); **~** v transfer (change trains/flights)

le costume suit

la côte rib (body part)

le coton cotton
la couche diaper
[nappy BE]
la couchette berth
le coude elbow
la couleur color
le couloir aisle
(plane)
le cou neck
le coup de soleil
sunburn
couper v cut
la coupure bill [note
BE] (money); **~** cut
(injury)
le courrier mail
[post BE]; **~ recom-
mandé** registered
mail
court short
le coût charge (cost)
le couteau knife
coûter v cost
le couvert cover
charge (restaurant)
la couverture
blanket
la cravate tie
(clothing)
la crème cream/
lotion; **~ antisep-
tique** antiseptic
cream; **~ solaire**
sunscreen
le cristal crystal
la cuillère spoon; **~
à café** teaspoon; **~
à doser** measuring
spoon
le cuir leather
la cuisine kitchen
cuisiner v cook
la cuisse thigh
le cuivre copper

les culottes panties
le cyber café internet
café

D

dangereux dangerous
dans in
dansant dancing
danser v dance
la date date
(calendar)
de nuit overnight
de rien you're
welcome
**le déboucheur de
toilettes** plunger
le débutant beginner
déclarer v declare
décoller v take off
(plane)
déconnecter discon-
nect (computer)
le degré degree
(temperature)
dehors outside
le déjeuner lunch
délicieux delicious
demain tomorrow
démarrer v start (an
automobile)
demi half; **~-heure**
half hour; **~-kilo**
half-kilo
la dent tooth
la dentelle lace
le dentier denture
le dentifrice
toothpaste
le dentiste dentist
le déodorant
deodorant
la dépanneuse tow
truck
les départs depar-

tures (airport)
déposer v deposit
le dépôt deposit
(bank)
dernier last
derrière behind
descendre v get
off (a train, bus,
subway)
le désert desert
désolé sorry
le détergent
detergent; **~ pour
lave-vaisselle**
dishwashing
liquid
développer v develop
(film)
la déviation alternate
route
diabétique diabetic
le diamant diamond
la diarrhée diarrhea
difficile difficult
dîner v dine; **le ~**
dinner
la direction direction
la discothèque
dance club
disparu missing
disponible available
le disquaire music
store
**le distributeur
automatique de
billets** automatic
teller machine (ATM)
le divertissement
entertainment
divorcer v divorce
le docteur doctor
le doigt finger
le dollar dollar (U.S.)
donner v give

dormir v sleep
le dortoir dormitory
le dos back (body
part)
la douane customs
doublé dubbed
la douche shower
la douleur hurt, pain;
~ à la poitrine
chest pain
la douzaine dozen
le drap sheet
droit straight; **~
d'entrée** cover
charge (bar, club)
du quartier local
DVD DVD

E

l'eau water; **~
chaude** hot water;
~ de Cologne
cologne; **~ potable**
drinking water
**l'échange de
monnaie** currency
exchange
échanger v change
(money)
l'échantillon
specimen
l'écharpe scarf
l'école school
les écouteurs
headphones
l'écran solaire
sunblock
écrire v text (send a
message); **~** v write
effacer v clear (on
an ATM)
l'effet secondaire
side effect
l'effraction break-in

(burglary)

égaliser v trim (hair cut)

l'église church

l'émail enamel (jewelry)

emballer v wrap

embarquer v board

embrasser v kiss

emporter to go [take away BE] (food order)

en sécurité safe (protected)

encaisser v cash

enceinte pregnant

endommagé damaged

l'enfant child

enlacer v hug

ennuyant boring

l'enregistrement check-in (hotel, airport)

enregistrer v check (luggage)

ensoleillé sunny

l'entorse sprain

l'entrée admission; ~ appetizer [starter BE]; ~ entrance

entrer v enter

l'enveloppe envelope

envoyer v send, ship; ~ **un fax** v fax; ~ **un mail** v e-mail

l'épaule shoulder

épeler v spell

épicé hot (spicy)

l'épilation à la cire du maillot bikini wax

l'épilation à la cire des sourcils

eyebrow wax

épileptique epileptic

l'épouse wife

épuisé exhausted

l'équipe team

l'équipement equipment; ~ **de plongée** diving/snorkeling equipment

l'erreur mistake

l'escalator escalators

les escaliers stairs

escarpé steep

ennuyer v bother

l'essence gas

l'essence petrol

est east

l'esthéticienne manicurist

l'estomac stomach

et and

l'étain pewter

l'étang pond

l'état de santé condition (medical); ~ **le problème cardiaque** heart condition

les États-Unis United States (U.S.)

éteindre v turn off (lights)

l'étiquette baggage ticket

étrange strange

être v be

l'étudiant student

étudier v study

l'euro euro

l'éventail fan (souvenir)

l'évier sink

l'excès excess

l'excursion excursion

excuser v excuse

l'expert expert (skill level)

l'express express

extra extra

F

facile easy

la facture bill [invoice BE]

faim hungry

faire v make, do; ~ **des achats** v shop; ~ **de l'auto stop** v hitchhike; ~ **les bagages** v pack; ~ **les courses** shopping; ~ **le plein** v fill; se ~ **réveiller par téléphone** wake-up call; ~ **du tourisme** sightseeing; ~ **du vélo** cycling; ~ **de la vitesse** speeding

faire un virement v transfer (money)

la falaise cliff

la famille family

le fast-food fast food

fatigué tired

le fax fax

la femme woman

la fenêtre window

le fer à repasser n iron (clothes)

fermé closed

la ferme farm

fermer v close, lock

le ferry ferry

les fesses buttocks

le feu fire; ~ **tricolore** traffic light

fiancé engaged

la fièvre fever

la fille girl

le film movie

finir v end

la fleur flower

le foie liver (body part)

la fontaine fountain

le football soccer [football BE]

la forêt forest; ~ **vierge** rainforest

le forfait lift pass

le formulaire form

le fort fort

la fourchette fork

frais cool (temperature); ~ **fresh**

français French

la France France

les freins brakes (car)

le frère brother

froid cold (temperature)

fumer v smoke

G

le garage garage, parking garage

garer v park

le garçon boy

la gare train [railway BE] station

la gare routière bus station

gay gay

le gaz cooking gas

la gazinière stove

le gazole diesel

le gel gel (hair)
le genou knee
le gilet de sauvetage life jacket
glacé icy
la glace ice
gonfler v swell
la gorge canyon; ~ throat
goûter v taste
la goutte drop (medicine)
le gramme gram
grand large
le grand magasin department store
grande taille plus size
les grands-parents grandparent
graver v engrave
gris gray
le groupe group
la gueule de bois hangover
le guide guide, guidebook
la gym gym
le gynécologue gynecologist

H

l'handicapé handicapped [disabled BE]
haut high
hebdomadaire weekly
l'hectare hectare
l'hétérosexuel heterosexual
l'heure hour
les heures d'ouverture business/office hours

les heures de visite visiting hours
heureux happy
hier yesterday
le hockey hockey; ~ sur glace ice hockey
l'homme man
l'hôpital hospital
l'horaire schedule [timetable BE]
hors taxe duty-free
l'hôtel hotel
l'huile oil

I

l'ibuprofène ibuprofen
ici here
l'identification identification
l'imperméable raincoat
imprimer v print
inclure v include
inconscient unconscious
infecté infected
l'infection vaginale vaginal infection
l'infirmier nurse
informer v notify
l'insecte bug
insérer v insert
l'insolation sunstroke
l'insomnie insomnia
l'insuline insulin
interdire v prohibit
intéressant interesting
l'international (terminal) international (airport area)

l'internet internet; ~ sans fil wireless internet
l'interprète interpreter
l'intersection intersection
l'intestin intestine
irlandais Irish
l'Irlande Ireland
l'irritation cutanée rash
italien Italian

J

la jambe leg
le jardin botanique botanical garden
jaune yellow
le jazz jazz
le jean jeans
jean denim
jetable disposable
le jeu game
jeune young
joindre v join
jouer v play
le jouet toy
le jour day
le journal newspaper
la jupe skirt

K

le kilo kilo; ~gramme kilogram; ~métrage mileage; ~mètre kilometer; ~mètre carré square kilometer
le kiosque à journaux newsstand
les Kleenex tissue

L

le lac lake
laid ugly
la laine wool
le lait pour bébés formula (baby)
la lame de rasoir razor blade
la lampe torche flashlight
la langue tongue
la laque hairspray
la laverie automatique laundromat [launderette BE]
le lave-vaisselle dishwasher
la leçon lesson
lentement slowly
les lentilles de contact contact lens
la lessive laundry
la lettre letter
les lèvres lip
la librairie bookstore
libre free; ~ vacancy
le lieu n place; ~ commémoratif memorial (place); ~ saint shrine; ~ touristique attraction (place)
la ligne line (train)
la lime à ongle nail file
la lingette pour bébé baby wipe
le lin linen
le liquide n cash
le lit bed; ~ double double bed; ~ pliant cot
le litre liter
le livre book

la livre sterling pounds (British sterling)

le logement accommodation

loin far

long long

la lotion anti-insectes insect repellent

louer v rent [hire BE]

la lumière light (overhead)

les lunettes glasses; **~ de soleil** sunglasses

M

la machine à laver washing machine

la mâchoire jaw

le magasin store; **~ de chaussures** shoe store; **~ de jouets** toy store; **~ de produits diététiques** health food store; **~ de souvenirs** souvenir store **~ de sport** sporting goods store; **~ de vêtements** clothing store; **~ de vins et spiritueux** liquor store

le magazine magazine

magnifique magnificent

le mail e-mail

le maillot de bain swimsuit

la main hand

maintenant now

la maison house

le mal sickness; **~ de l'air** motion -sickness (air); **~ de dos** backache; **~ de gorge** sore throat; **~ de mer** motion sickness (sea); **~ de tête** headache; **~ des transports** travel sickness

malade ill, sick

les maladies sexuellement transmissibles sexually transmitted disease (STD)

malvoyant visually impaired

les manches courtes short sleeves

les manches longues long sleeves

manger v eat

le manteau coat

la manucure manicure

le marchand de fruits et légumes produce store

le marchand de vins et de spiritueux liquor store [off-licence BE]

le marché market

marcher v walk

le mari husband

marié married

la mairie town hall

se marier v marry

marron brown

le marteau hammer

le massage massage

le match n match; **~ de boxe** boxing match; **~ de football** soccer [football BE] game; **~ de volleyball** volleyball game

le matin morning

le maux de ventre stomachache

le mécanicien mechanic

le médicament medicine

meilleur best

le même same

le menu menu; **~ enfant** children's menu

la mer sea

merci thank you

la mère mother

le message message; **~ instantané** instant message

la messe mass (church service)

la mesure measuring cup

mesurer to measure (someone)

la météo forecast

le mètre carré square meter

le métro subway [underground BE]

le micro-onde microwave

midi noon [midday BE]

mieux better

mignon cute

le mini bar mini-bar

minuit midnight

la minute minute

le mobile home mobile home

la mobilité mobility

la mobylette moped

les mocassins loafers

modifier v alter

moins less; **~ cher** cheaper

le mois month

la moitié half

la monnaie n change (money); **~ currency**

la montagne mountain

la montre watch

montrer v show

le morceau piece

la mosquée mosque

le mot de passe password

la moto motorcycle

la mousse mousse; **~ à raser** shaving cream

moyen medium (size)

le muscle muscle

le musée museum

la musique music; **~ classique** classical music; **~ folklorique** folk music

myope near- [short-BE] sighted

N

nager v swim

national domestic

la nationalité nationality

neigeux snowy

nettoyer v clean
le nez nose
le night club nightclub
le niveau intermédiaire intermediate
noir black
le nom name; ~ **de l'utilisateur** username
non no; ~ **alcoolisé** non-alcoholic; ~ **fumeur** non-smoking
nord north
nourrir v feed
le novice novice (skill level)
de nuit overnight
la nuit night
numérique digital
le numéro number; ~ **de fax** fax number; ~ **de permis de conduire** driver's license -number; ~ **de téléphone** phone number

O

les objets trouvés lost and found
l'œil eye
l'oiseau bird
l'ongle fingernail, toenail
l'opéra opera
l'opticien optician
l'or gold; ~ **blanc** white gold; ~ **jaune** yellow gold
orange orange (color)
l'orchestre orchestra
ordinaire regular

l'ordinateur computer
l'ordonnance prescription
les ordures à recycler recycling
l'oreille ear
l'oreiller pillow
l'orteil toe
l'os bone
l'otite earache
où where
ouest west
oui yes
ouvert open
l'ouvre-bouteille/boîte bottle/can opener
ouvrir v open; ~ **une session** v log on (computer)

P

le palais palace
le palais des congrès convention hall
le panier basket (grocery store)
la panne breakdown
le pansement bandage
le pantalon pants [trousers BE]
le papier paper; ~ **aluminium** aluminum [kitchen BE] foil; ~ **toilette** toilet paper
le paquet carton
par by; ~ **avion** airmail; ~ **heure** per hour; ~ **jour** per day; ~ **nuit** per night; ~ **semaine** per week

le paracétamol acetaminophen [paracetamol BE]
le parapluie umbrella
le parc playpen; ~ **park**; ~ **d'attractions** amusement park
le parfum perfume
parier to place (a bet)
le parking parking lot [car park BE]
parler v speak
participer v attend
pas cher inexpensive
le passager passenger
le passeport passport
passer v pass through
la passoire colander
la pataugeoire kiddie pool
la pâtisserie pastry shop
payer v pay; ~ **par carte** v charge (credit card)
la peau skin
le pédiatre pediatrician
la pédicure pedicure
le peigne comb
la pellicule film (camera)
pendant during
la pendule wall clock
la pénicilline penicillin
le pénis penis
perdre v lose (something)
perdu lost
le père father

la période period (of time)
la perle pearl
permettre v allow
la perte discharge (bodily fluid)
petit small
le petit child, small; ~-**ami** boyfriend; ~-**amie** girlfriend; ~ **déjeuner** breakfast
les petits-enfants grandchildren
peu little
la pharmacie pharmacy [chemist BE]
la photo photo; ~**copie** photocopy; ~**graphie** photography; ~ **numérique** digital photo
la pièce coin; ~ **part** (for car); ~ n **play** (theater); ~ **room**
le pied foot
le piéton pedestrian
la pile battery
le pilier tent pole
la pilule Pill (birth control)
le piquet tent peg
la piqûre sting; ~ **d'insecte** insect bite
la piscine pool; ~ **intérieure** indoor pool; ~ **extérieure** outdoor pool
la piste trail [piste BE]; ~ **cyclable** bike route
la pizzeria pizzeria
la plage beach

la plainte complaint
le plaisir pleasure
le plan du magasin store directory
le plat principal main course
platine platinum
le plombage filling (tooth)
plonger v dive
la pluie rain
plus more; ~ **bas** lower; ~ **fort** louder; ~ **grand** larger; ~ **lent** slower; ~ **petit** smaller; ~ **tard** later; ~ **tôt** earlier; ~ **vite** faster
pluvieux rainy
le pneu tire [tyre BE]; ~ **crevé** flat tire [tyre BE]
la poche pocket
la poêle frying pan
le poignet wrist
le point d'observation overlook [viewpoint BE] (scenic place)
le poison poison
la poitrine chest (body part)
la police police
la pompe à air air pump
les pompiers fire department
le pont bridge
la pop musique pop music
le portable wireless/ cell [mobile BE] phone

la porte gate (airport); ~ door; ~ **coupe-feu** fire door
le portefeuille wallet
la portion portion; ~ **enfant** children's portion
la pose exposure (film)
le poste extension (phone)
le pot jar
la poterie pottery
la poubelle garbage [rubbish BE]
le poumon lung
la poupée doll
pour for
pourpre purple
pousser to push (door sign)
la poussette stroller [pushchair BE]
précieux valuable
premier first
la première classe first class
prendre v pick up (something); ~ v take; ~ **plaisir** v enjoy; ~ **sa retraite** retired
près close, near; ~ **de** nearby
presbyte far- [long- BE] sighted
prescrire to prescribe
présenter v introduce
le préservatif condom
prévoir v schedule
la principale at- traction

touristique main attraction
la prise électrique electric outlet
le prix price
le problème problem
produire produce
le produit product; ~ **d'entretien** cleaning product; ~ **ménager** household good
profondément deeply
la promenade walk
prononcer v pronounce
propre clean
public public
le pull sweater
le pyjama pajamas

Q

le quai n track [plat- form BE] (train)
la qualité quality
quand when
le quartier des magasins shop- ping area
la question question
qui who
quitter la chambre check-out (hotel)
quoi what

R

raccourcir v to shorten
la rampe d'accès wheelchair ramp
le rap rap (music)
le rapport de police police report
la raquette racket (sports)

le rasoir jetable disposable razor
la réaction allergique allergic reaction
la réception recep- tion
recevoir v receive
recharger v recharge
le réchaud camping stove
réchauffer v warm (something)
recommandation recommendation
recommander v recommend
le reçu n bill, receipt (of sale)
recycler recycling
la réduction discount
le réfrigérateur refrigerator
refuser v decline (credit card)
regarder v look
la région region
les règles period (menstrual)
les règles douloureuses menstrual cramps
le rein kidney (body part)
la relation relation- ship
remercier v thank
le remonte-pentes drag lift
la remorque trailer
remplir v fill out (form)
rencontrer v meet (someone)

le rendez-vous appointment

rendre v return (something)

les renseignements information (phone)

réparer v fix (repair)

le repas meal

repasser v iron

répéter v repeat

la réservation reservation

la réserve naturelle nature preserve

réserver v reserve

le résident européen EU resident

respirer v breathe

le responsable manager

le restaurant restaurant

rester v stay

retarder v delay

retirer v withdraw

le retrait withdrawal (bank); **~ des bagages** baggage claim

la réunion meeting

réveiller v wake

le rez-de-chaussée ground floor

le rhume cold (sickness)

rien anything, nothing

la rivière river

la robe dress (piece of clothing)

romantique romantic

rose pink

rouge red

la route route

le Royaume Uni United Kingdom (U.K.)

le rugby rugby

les ruines ruins

le ruisseau stream

S

s'asseoir v sit

s'il vous plaît please

le sac bag, purse; **~à dos** backpack; **~ à appareil photo** camera case; **~ de couchage** sleeping bag; **~ à main** purse [handbag BE]; **~ poubelle** garbage [rubbish BE] bag

le sachet bag

saigner v bleed

le saladier bowl

sale dirty

la salle room: **~ d'attente** waiting room; **~ de concert** concert hall; **~ à manger** dining room; **~ de réunion** meeting room

le salon d'essayage fitting room

salut hi

les sandales sandals

le sang blood

sans without; **~ 0% de matières grasses** fat free; **~ ordonnance** over the counter (medication); **~ plomb** unleaded (gasoline); **~ surveillance** unattended

la santé health

Santé! Cheers!

le sauna sauna

sauvegarder v save (computer)

le savon soap

le scanner scanner

la science science

le sèche-cheveux hair dryer

le secouriste lifeguard

la sécurité security

le sein breast

le self-service self-service

la semaine week

le séminaire seminar

les seniors senior citizens

le sens unique one-way street

séparé separated (marriage)

sérieux serious

la serpillière mop; ~ groundcloth

le serveur waiter

la serveuse waitress

le service service (in a restaurant); **~ de chambre** room service; **~ complet** full-service; **~ d'entretien** housekeeping services; **~ internet** internet service; **~ de nettoyage** laundry service

la serviette napkin, towel; **~ hygiénique** sanitary napkin

[pad BE]

seul alone

seulement only

le shampooing shampoo

le short shorts

le siège seat; **~ bébé** car seat; **~ couloir** aisle seat; **~ enfant** child's seat

signer v sign

le silence quiet

le ski ski; **~ jet** jet ski

skier v ski

les skis nautiques water skis

les slips briefs [underpants BE] (clothing)

le snowboard snowboard

la sœur sister

la soie silk

soif thirsty

le soin à l'oxygène oxygen treatment

le soin du visage facial

la soirée evening

le sol floor

le soleil sun

la solution pour lentilles de contact contact lens solution

sombre dark

le sommet peak

somnolence drowsiness

la serviette en papier paper towel

la sortie exit; **~ de secours** emergency

exit

sortir to exit

la source chaude hot spring

sourd deaf

les sous-vêtements underwear

le soutien-gorge bra

le souvenir souvenir

le spa spa

la spatule spatula

le spécialiste specialist (doctor)

le sport sports

le stade stadium

la station station; **~ de métro** subway [underground BE] station; **~ service** gas [petrol BE] station

la statue statue

stupéfiant stunning

le style de coiffure hairstyle

le stylo pen

subtil subtitle

sucré sweet (taste)

sud south

suivant next

le super super (fuel)

supérieur upper

le supermarché supermarket

la supervision supervision

supprimer v delete (computer)

le surf surfboard

surprenant amazing

le sweat-shirt sweatshirt

le symbole symbol

(keyboard)

la synagogue synagogue

le syndicat d'initiative tourist information office

le Syndrome d'immuno-déficience acquise (SIDA) AIDS

T

le tabac tobacconist

la table table

la taille size

le tampon tampon

frapper v (computer) type

le tapis de sol groundcloth

tard late (time)

la tasse cup

le taux de change exchange rate

la taxe duty (tax)

le taxi taxi

la teinturerie dry cleaner

la télé TV; **~le téléphérique** cable car; **~le téléphone** phone; **~le téléphone public** pay phone

téléphoner v phone

le télésiège chair lift

le temple temple (religious)

temporaire temporary

le temps time, weather; **~ partiel** part-time; **~ plein** full-time

le tennis tennis

les tennis sneakers

la tension blood pressure

la tente tent

la tenue exigée dress code

le terminal terminal (airport)

terminer une session v log off (computer)

le terrain field, course; **~ de golf** golf course

la terre cuite terracotta

terrible terrible

la tête head (body part)

la tétine pacifier [soother BE]

le texte text (message)

le théâtre theater

le ticket ticket; **~ de bus** bus ticket

le timbre stamp (postage)

le tirage unique single prints

le tire-bouchon corkscrew

tirer v pull (door sign)

les toilettes restroom [toilet BE]

les toilettes portables chemical toilet

tôt early

total total (amount)

la tour tower

le touriste tourist

le tournoi de golf golf tournament

tousser v cough

tout de suite right of way

la toux cough

traditionnel traditional

traduire v translate

le train train

tranchant sharp

la tranche slice

travailler v work

très grand extra large

triste sad

trop too

le t-shirt T-shirt

la TVA sales tax [VAT BE]

U

un one

une fois once

l'université university

l'urgence emergency

urgent urgent

l'ustensile utensil

les produits d'entretien cleaning supplies

utiliser v use

V

les vacances vacation [holiday BE]

la vaccination vaccination

le vagin vagina

la vaisselle dish (kitchen)

la valeur value

valide valid

la valise suitcase

la vallée valley
végétarien vegetarian
le véliplanchiste windsurfer
le vélo tout terrain (VTT) mountain bike
vendre v sell
venir v come
le ventilateur fan (appliance)
vérifier v check (on something)
le verre glass, lens
vert green
la vessie bladder
la veste jacket
les vêtements clothing

le veuf widowed
vider v empty
vieux old
le vignoble vineyard
le village village
la ville town
le viol rape
violer v rape
le visage face
la visite tour; **~ en bus** bus tour
la visite touristique sightseeing tour
visiter v visit
la vitamine vitamin
vite fast
la vitrine display case

vivre v live
voir v see
la voiture car; **~ automatique** automatic car; **~ de location** car rental [hire BE]; **~ de location** rental [hire BE] car; **~ manuelle** manual car
le vol flight; **~ national** domestic flight; **~ international** international flight
volé stolen
voler v rob, steal
le voleur thief

vomir v vomit
le voyage trip
vrai real

W

le wagon couchette sleeper [sleeping BE] car
le week-end weekend
wireless internet wireless internet service

Z

la zone fumeur smoking (area)
le zoo zoo

INDEX

Berlitz pocket guide

NICE, CANNES & MONTE CARLO

Fourth Edition 2019

Editor: Zara Sekhavati
Author: Natasha Foges
Head of DTP and Pre-Press: Rebeka Davies
Managing Editor: Carine Tracanelli
Picture Editor: Tom Smyth
Cartography Update: Carte
Update Production: Apa Digital
Photography Credits: Fotolia 37, 88;
Getty Images 20, 23, 79, 90; iStock
4TC, 4ML, 4TL, 5MC, 26, 40, 62, 69,
71, 80, 81, 84, 99, 102, 104; Norbert
Scanella/Onlyfrance/4Corners Images
1; Peter Stuckings/Apa Publications 6L;
Shutterstock 5T, 5M, 5MC, 5M, 11, 15,
18, 33, 54, 61, 95; Sylvaine Poitau/APA
Publications 4MC, 5TC, 6R, 7, 7R, 13, 17,
28, 31, 34, 38, 43, 45, 47, 48, 51, 52, 57, 58,
65, 66, 73, 75, 77, 87, 91, 93, 96, 100; Wadey
James/Apa Publications 82
Cover Picture: Susanne Kremer/4Corners
Images

Distribution
UK, Ireland and Europe: Apa Publications
(UK) Ltd; sales@insightguides.com
United States and Canada: Ingram
Publisher Services; ips@ingramcontent.com
Australia and New Zealand: Woodslane;
info@woodslane.com.au
Southeast Asia: Apa Publications (SN) Pte;
singaporeoffice@insightguides.com
Worldwide: Apa Publications (UK) Ltd;
sales@insightguides.com

**Special Sales, Content Licensing
and CoPublishing**
Insight Guides can be purchased in bulk
quantities at discounted prices. We can
create special editions, personalised jackets
and corporate imprints tailored to your
needs. sales@insightguides.com;
www.insightguides.biz

Contact us
Every effort has been made to provide
accurate information in this publication,
but changes are inevitable. The publisher
cannot be responsible for any resulting loss,
inconvenience or injury. We would appreciate
it if readers would call our attention to any
errors or outdated information. We also
welcome your suggestions; please contact
us at: berlitz@apaguide.co.uk
www.insightguides.com/berlitz